Catherine McCann

Time-Out In Shekina

The Value Of Symbols
In Our Search For Meaning

Eleona Books

'No man can reveal to you aught but that which already lies half asleep in the dawning of your knowledge.

The teacher who walks in the shadow of the temple..., gives not of his wisdom but rather of his faith and his lovingness.

If he is indeed wise he does not bid you enter the house of his wisdom, but leads you to the threshold of your own mind'.

Kahil Gibran, in The Prophet

This book is dedicated to all seekers of truth, beauty, love, wisdom.

Time-Out in Shekina attempts to awaken you to the song in your own heart.

First published, 1998, by

ELEONA BOOKS

42 Donnybrook Manor, Dublin 4.

Ph/ Fax 353 1 2838711.

Design by Creative Inputs

Photography by Con Brogan of Duchas

Printed by McDonald and Glennon

ISBN 0 9531302 2 3

Acknowledgement: John O'Donohue 1997. Extracts from ANAM CARA published by Bantam Press, a division of Transworld Publishers Ltd. All rights reserved.

OUTLINE

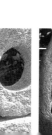

Introduction

Time-Out means taking time for ourselves. It involves moving out of our normal routine and at times out of our normal environment. We do this for many reasons; we take time-out for play, for education, for relaxation. In this context it means taking time-out for personal reflection in order to get in touch with our deepest selves. The way we achieve this is by being alert and open to the on-going quest for deeper meaning that presents itself as we live out our human existence. Put differently, it is about awakening or rediscovering the spiritual part of ourselves; that dimension of our humanity which makes us profoundly human.

Spirituality and the search for meaning are one and the same reality. Some of us suffer from a degree of spiritual malnutrition due to our inner life receiving inadequate attention. This is often due to the pace and noise of modern living which leaves little room for reflection and stillness, something true even for young children. Not being able to make time to reflect on what lies deepest in us can lead to apathy and even to meaninglessness in personal living. Living with a level of meaning that satisfies comes from discovering our inner hopes and desires. That is what spirituality, the life of the human spirit, is about.

Being in touch with these desires can lead to a religious quest when the search for ultimate meaning, particularly concerning our origin and destiny, become important issues. Religion is the formalising of spirituality into systems. These systems flow from a central realization which acknowledges that human life is dependant on a power greater than itself. Authentic religious values and practice spring from personal spiritual awareness. True understanding and practice of religion is not a confining experience as some people think. When religious belief is genuine it leads more and more to an experience of liberation. Central to Christianity, for instance, are Jesus' words where he said he came to set people free (See Jn 8:36).

Time-Out in Shekina offers an opportunity to get in touch with the profounder realities of human life. *Shekina Sculpture Garden* is a place which can prove valuable since it opens people,

through the sculptural symbols it contains, to the value of symbols in our search for wisdom.[1]

Shekina is a Hebrew word that denotes the presence of God among his people, namely the whole human family. It also carries with it the added note of God's presence being experienced in particular places. Time-Out in this garden can heighten awareness of God's presence but God's presence can be found everywhere so the Time-Out experience offered in this book can be done in the privacy of your home, garden or anywhere you choose. Two particular ways of making such Time-Out reflections are to ponder the text when visiting this garden or, alternatively, to read the text anywhere, alongside your viewing the illustration of the sculpture which is shown at the beginning of each reflection.

You can also simply read the text on its own, or, relate the text to other symbols that speak to you. Yet another way would be to create your own symbols. Examples of symbols that might be used could be taken from nature; personal photographs or other memorabilia concerned with your own life story; personal drawings; or other creative forms of expression that might be elicited in you as you read the text.

Symbols are a powerful means of enhancing our personal understanding of reality. In this work the focus of our understanding is *The Mystery of God* and the rich relational life that exists between Father, Son and Spirit and *The Mystery of the Human Person* and the fundamental aspects of human living such as relationships, (pondering in particular the core relationships between parent and child, lovers, and within community), and questions concerning death and what lies beyond it.

The lay-out of each reflection is the same. It is suggested that you use this format in the following way. First look at the sculpture or the illustration of it - or your alternative symbol - and ponder what it says to you. Following that read the input which begins with some thoughts on what the sculpture might evoke. Then read the rest of the text which offers a

---

[1] The Meaning of Symbols section in the appendix throws light on the text as a whole. It could prove helpful to read this part towards the beginning, rather than leave it to the end.

more in depth reflection on the central theme suggested by the sculpture. Finally reflect again on what insights, feelings and desires become present in yourself. Reflection questions conclude each section. These questions or comments are not intended to take from your own questioning, but are given to augment your own reflections should that be necessary.

Each of the twelve sculptures has its own reflection. While the sculptures are set out in a particular order so that the unfolding of the creation story is kept to the fore, you can start anywhere since each reflection is a unit in itself. For instance you may be drawn to begin with the Creation of Man and Woman, or the Mystery of Jesus or whatever topic attracts your attention. Each reflection offers challenge - some stretch at the intellectual level, especially the first four, others at the emotional, and most offer spiritual challenge.

The sculptures evoke the story of creation as understood by the Hebrew/Christian tradition. The first sculpture begins with ourselves - the Mystery of the Human Person. The story then moves to Absolute Mystery - God who is symbolized in the second sculpture. The third sculpture focuses on the Holy Spirit, followed by one on the Creation of the Universe and then the fifth on the Creation of Man and Woman. The sixth sculpture takes up the theme of Childhood and is followed by two others which focus on the basic relationships of adult life, namely with Significant Others and on Community. The last three are on Death, Jesus and Eternity. Shekina Sculpture Garden is the context in which the creation story is told so the garden forms the basis for the final reflection. All the reflections are coloured by a Christian ethos since Christianity is the faith professed by the author.

The reflections draw on the findings of science, psychology, philosophy and theology. The overall aim is to awaken and deepen our knowledge of the Mystery of the Human and the Mystery of God. When the relationship between God and ourselves results in a meeting we are at prayer. Hopefully an outcome of these reflections is that they will lead to a more authentic prayer life.

The dispositions required as a person embarks on this Time-Out are openness, awareness,

flexibility, and a preparedness to alter or let go attitudes and thinking patterns that might be overly rigid, hard and certain. It is above all about widening horizons. For instance there is always need to challenge ourselves about our image of God as well as our image of ourselves. Is our image of both too narrow, too limited? Our image of God will always be limited since we are created beings but it is important to allow that image to change as new insights/experiences occur over life. To hold onto childhood or fundamentalist images of God is unhelpful and diminishes both ourselves and God. Such images are unable to provide sufficient meaning and nourishment that will make a difference to our lives; the kind of meaning that helps to sustain us particularly as we undergo suffering of all kinds.

Our image of ourselves can also be distorted if we fail to see the true greatness of the human person; the true greatness of who we are. The mystery of who we are now is the result of our own personal history. Owning our story, the painful as well as the joyfilled parts, allows us to live the present more fully. It also helps us to face the future with a hope that is life-giving. These reflections offer an opportunity to reflect on our own creation story as well as God's story of creation.

It is important to note that while Time-out experiences are for personal growth and relaxation they are not individualistic happenings. Self-development, getting in touch with our deeper self, enhances not only ourselves; the enrichment gained will inevitably affect those we are close to, those with whom we live or work, as well as the wider community. The beneficiaries of our time-out moments can be far-reaching and benefits may arise that we could never have envisaged.

The Mystery of the Human Person

Sculpture

Fred Conlon's work is, as he says, an invitation to question. Since the human person is essentially a mystery we find ourselves constantly questioning. This sculpture is therefore an appropriate symbol of the mystery of who we are. All through life we question: why, who, how, what, where, when, and we even at times question our own questioning. Fundamental questions are those which concern our origins and our destiny. Fred's questions concerning this piece include: 'Does the sculpture make an enquirer of you? How does the sculpture make you feel? Why does the sculpture have opposite harmonies and how does it have a cohesive unity?' He titles the piece *Ni Mar a Shiltear Bitear -Things are not what they seem*. The sculpture he says 'focuses on creating harmony of opposites and contradictions'.

These opposites are captured in the dots and stripes, the light and dark grey, the straight and curvy lines The centre of the piece is what strikes most - the circle that becomes a diamond, the diamond that becomes a circle.[2] Both are symbols of wholeness, richness and transparency. In this sculpture both shapes are expressed in cut-out form, and in a way that the diamond and circle are open to each other. Both too allow light to penetrate through. From which ever side we view the vista that lies before us, our image of that reality, namely our perspective on that vista, is bounded by the horizon of either the diamond or the circle. It is therefore a work whose centre is all about horizons.

This reflection centres on humanity's origins, personal origins, and the human person's capacity for transcendence.

Humanity's Origins

Richard Leakey, the palaeontologist says: 'as a species, we are blessed with a curiosity about the world of nature and our place in it. We want to know - *need* to know - how we came

---

[2] Unfortunately the view of the diamond is not visible in the illustration since it appears the reverse side of the sculpture.

to be and what our future is.'[3] Palaeontologists, anthropologists, archaeologists and more recently geneticists, try to date the origins of the human person and say that *Homo Sapiens* (i.e. people like us, not prototypes such as Homo Erectus or Apes) emerged somewhere between 100,000 - 50-000 years ago. Abraham the first historical biblical figure lived many millennia later, around 2,000 BC.

The fossils of the Qafzeh boy, found in Israel near Nazareth in 1987, are considered the oldest find of the human person. He was like us anatomically; the most significant features are the skull size, the pharynx, and the thumb, hip and knee joints. But what was this person like in behaviour? The gap between his date of approximately 70,000 BC and the existing evidence we have of human culture is 30,000 years. Of this period little is known. Some of the signs of early culture include paintings (in caves in the south of France) 40,000 BC, a sculpture 29,000 BC, cities (Jericho 10,000 BC) and the alphabet and therefore writing 6,000 BC.

Science works on factual questions, philosophy and religion focuses on the why questions and especially the why questions concerning ourselves and God. Religious questions often emerge from, as well as evoke, a sense of awe and wonder. (See Ps 8: 3-6)

Personal Origins

Our existence is imposed on us; we were born without being consulted. We cannot step out of our existence. The terrible, awesome reality is that it is impossible for us not to be. However the fact that we exist does not mean that we consciously accept our existence as it was, as it is today and as it will turn out for us. None of us will have accepted this truth wholeheartedly in all its dimensions.

There are many personal 'givens' such as our genetic makeup, bodily characteristics, intellectual ability, and emotional functioning. The choice remains open as to whether we love or hate the One who imposed our existence on us. The decision is ours as to whether, according to Rahner, we accept our existence as 'the marvel of love', or reject it in protest.

[3] R. Leakey, The Origin of Humankind, (London: Phoenix 1995) xv.

Part of accepting the marvel of being chosen to exist is taken further by Paul who says we were chosen for a purpose (see Eph 1: 4,5). Jesus states that purpose clearly: Live Life Fully, 'I have come that you may have life and have it to the full' (Jn 10:10). Living life fully and bearing fruit, Jesus says, means developing our talents and using our gifts,[4] as well as taking up the opportunities that come our way. 'To him whom much is given, much will be expected in return' (Lk 12:48).

Living a full human life means attending to and developing the physical, intellectual, emotional, and spiritual dimensions of our person. For instance do we take reasonable care of our bodies? Do we stretch our intellects sufficiently? Do we live in depth and grow through the variety of our emotional experiences? Do we sensitively listen to and do something about our deepest desires?

Living our deepest desires is closely linked with the whole question of the human person's search for meaning. This search is always on-going.

Meaning to life is a foundational question

V. Frankl[5], a German psychiatrist, reminds us that the meaning question concerns not just life in general, but more importantly that we find meaning to life as we live it concretely each day. 'Striving to find a meaning in one's life is the primary motivational force in man'. The principle of his 'Logotherapy' was to help clients find a meaning to their lives. He feels today many, both young and old, lack the awareness of a meaning worth living for.

When we moved from the animal world we lost the security of instinct and moved to a world of choice where instinct no longer dictates to us what we have to do. This century we are aware of two extreme paths that people take. There are those we follow what others do - conformism; or those who follow what others insist they do - totalitarianism. The path modern culture takes is to discard many traditions which formally buttressed acceptable

---

4 See the parable of the talents. (Mt 25:14-30).
5 All quotations in this section are taken from V. Frankl, *Man's Search for Meaning* (New York: Washington Square Press 1946).

patterns of behaviour. As a result our present culture requires a more demanding form of life in the sense that more personal choice becomes necessary. Such choices must be meaning-filled if life is to be fulfilling.

Distress and boredom are two indicators of lack of meaning in life. Frankl illustrates this well in what he terms the 'Sunday neurosis' phenomena. By this he means the boredom and anxiety that arises in people when they have free time and do not know what to do with it.

Finding meaning in suffering is the ultimate task; facing a fate that cannot be changed entails changing a tragedy into something that has positive meaning. 'Suffering ceases to be suffering at the moment it finds a meaning, such as the meaning of a sacrifice' according to Frankl. In his own life Frankl lost his precious text in the concentration camp. He discovered the challenge then was 'to *live* my thoughts instead of putting them on paper.' We are never so trapped or determined that we are no longer free to make choices about how we stand before difficult conditions. We are self-determining beings - we can behave like swine or saints. A famous quote of his is: 'Today people have enough to live *by*, but not enough to live *for*'.

The search for meaning and the desire to live life fully is most fully satisfied when we allow ourselves be open to receive the fullness of life itself - God. 'Knowing the love of Christ, which is beyond all knowledge, you are filled with the utter fullness of God' (Eph 3:19).

The Human Person's Capacity for Transcendence[6]

Our awareness of the presence of good and evil, progress and decline causes us to inquire. Our intelligence drives us to know why, what, how. We are not satisfied until we reach some form of reasonable answer. The fact that we seek at all implies that the universe is intelligible, and 'once that is granted, there arises the question whether the universe could be intelligible without having an intelligible ground'.[7] That is the God question. A particular problem today

---

[6] Transcendence can be defined as our ability to reach beyond ourselves. We transcend ourselves for instance when we love and when we question.

[7] B. Lonergan, *Method in Theology* (Toronto: University of Toronto Press 1971) 101. Hereafter *Method*. Bernard Lonergan is a Canadian theologian.

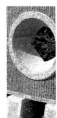

is that some people appear to have lost the sense of the questions to which the God question gives the sublime answer.[8]

As we reflect on the evidence we collect we are forced to make a judgement on the matter about which we are discerning; for example whether something is good or evil. Evidence forces us to take a stance: this is so, this is not so, this probably is or is not so. When we come to the God question, we have to discern whether a necessary being exists - a being that transcends all other forms of reality.

To help us further answer this question: consider how we search for value. We ask ourselves is this or that worthwhile when we make choices. We praise progress and denounce decline but on what basis? Are we just gamblers, guessers, in our search for the good or is there an intelligent ground of the universe? Is that intelligent ground, from which we make our choices, our own individual moral consciousness? This leads us to ask a more fundamental question: what is the source of our conscience? is it ourselves or something beyond ourselves?

The God question cannot be answered by the feelings, images, or thoughts we may at times try to muster up. The God question is a question not an answer. In other words we come to necessary being, the source of conscience, God, when we advert to our own questioning and question that questioning. The human spirit not only questions, but questions without restriction and it is through that activity that we come dimly to discern that something-greater-than-ourselves whom we name God.

Lonergan says 'the question of God then lies within man's horizons'.[9] Our constant drive is to discover what is intelligible, what is of value. We never fully attain this but it is *in our very reaching* that God can be discovered. Again Lonergan states,'there lies within his [the human

---

[8] D. Walsh, *After Ideology, Recovering the spiritual foundations of Freedom*, (San Fransisco: Harper 1990) 37. Walsh, an Irish theologian takes up another author and says: 'Voegelin has observed, that the problem with Christians today is not that they do not have the answer, but that they have lost the question to which it is the answer. ('The Gospel and Culture' in *Jesus and Man's Hope*)
[9] *Method*, 103.

person's] horizon a region for the divine, a shrine for ultimate holiness. It cannot be ignored. The atheist may pronounce it empty. The agnostic may urge that he finds his investigation has been inconclusive. The contemporary humanist will refuse to allow the question to arise. But their negations presuppose the spark in our clod, our native orientation to the divine.'[10]

We become authentic as human persons through transcending ourselves and we do this through our questioning. Not to question is to stay locked up in oneself. The core questions we ask relate to intelligibility which are answered in our minds, and the questions concerning value which are answered by our moral choices. Both forms of questioning show our transcendence, namely our ability to reach beyond ourselves. This ability becomes actuality when we act, for example when we perform the good act. The highest form of actualising our self-transcendence is when we love.

There are three forms of this love, the love of intimacy (close relationships), love of all people, love of God. Being in love with God, means being in love unrestrictedly. Being in love with God who is absolute mystery means that this type of love can only be described as an experience of mystery.

As we journey through life we become more aware of the many contradictions we find in ourselves. The wonder of our dignity and destiny is always coupled with our immense fragility. For instance, Paul says: 'I cannot understand my own behaviour. I fail to carry out the things I want to do, and I find myself doing the very things I hate (Rm 4:14). M. Kearney speaks of our inner contradictions as the lack of integration we experience at times in our deepest self; when our outer self, the ways we live our lives outwardly, is not in tune or at one with what lies deepest in us; when our behaviour and general life style, are not in harmony with our deepest desires.[11]

---

[10] Ibid.
[11] Michael Kearney is a medical doctor who works in Palliative Care in Dublin. He is author of *Mortally Wounded, Stories of Soul Pain, Death and Healing* (Dublin: Marino Books 1996).

Reflection

Ponder on the mystery of yourself. Reflect not so much on 'who am I?' but 'who I am', namely on the uniqueness of your own person. Do you have faith in yourself? In your own greatness?

Reflect on your horizons; the boundaries you set when viewing yourself, God, and the whole of reality. Consider the possibility of expanding such horizons by returning to your fundamental gift - the ability to ask questions.

Get in touch with your longings, desires, especially your desire for truth, beauty, freedom, love.

The 'moreness' to life is always open to us. Do you desire it, leave yourself open to receive it through your questioning and loving?

Reflect on Psalm 139 and Psalm 8:3-6

Absolute Mystery - God

Sculpture

This sculpture expresses God as mystery. In this work Fred Conlon tries to convey a sense of strength and security coupled with a sense of great movement. This combination of differences is expressed in the single form which Fred has sculpted out of this large piece of granite. The spiral that has no beginning or end as well as the spiral's open-ended centre, hints at infinity. Allowing oneself to: be drawn into its dynamic centre; be supported and held in its womb-like curvature, can give a minuscule experience of living within the mystery of life and love, namely within the mystery of God.

People like touching this sculpture and especially sitting in it. It offers a sense of solid support while giving the sense of being wrapped, surrounded, enveloped... It invites a person to relax into the power and strength that this Mystery offers while this same Mystery never forces itself on us. It invites to a simple being there; a surrendering to what is.... It is a place to pose, to say this is me! me in my rightful place! Mystery is something warm, tender, womb-like, while also something strong... Absolute Mystery is total love loving totally. It is apt that this is the most dominant piece in the garden... it attempts to say so much.. to say what words are often inadequate to express...

Absolute Mystery - God is reflected on under the following headings: God - Absolute Mystery, Trinity of Persons, the Unity of God, Trinity as the Mystery of the Christian faith, and the person of God the Father.

God - Absolute Mystery [12]

Who is this God 'in whom', as Paul says 'we live, move and have our being'? (Acts 17:28).

The slogan 'God is dead' is fading. But a difficulty always remains: how do we speak about something which is beyond language? We can only ever hint at who God is. The danger is that

---

[12] By mystery is meant a truth which transcends the power of the human mind.

when we pin things down we can get further from the truth. Around 100 AD, John of Patmos, the author of the Book of Revelation gives God three titles: 'the Alpha and the Omega' (1:8), 'the One who is, who was and who is to come' (1:4) and 'the Lord God the Almighty' (1:8). Interestingly none of these titles have gender attached. Rahner, this century, describes God as follows: 'God is hidden, God is mystery, God is absolute mystery'.[13]

A constant problem is that a transcendent God may seem a distant God but transcendence describes difference not distance. The bible is insistent that God is close to his people and especially 'the brokenhearted' (Ps 34:18). The Christian understanding has always been that God emerges from hiddeness into history but in a way that God remains utterly beyond all that is created. God cannot become part of creation, yet often that is how people perceive God, especially pantheists. Neither is God someone who is super-human although there is the human tendancy to make God just that. We can image God as just 'another bit' of reality, another 'thing', another 'person'. This is not possible and that is why we cannot 'name' God. God is beyond human knowing.

For Rahner 'God is that blazing reality which is and remains with us Absolute Mystery'. For M. Buber, a German philosopher, God is fundamentally person, not a principle or an idea and this God 'enters into a direct relation with us men in creative, revealing and redemptive acts, and thus makes it possible for us to enter into a direct relation with him'.[14]

Through revelation, and especially through Jesus the mystery of God is made more radically present - but still as mystery. In fact the Incarnation deepens our perception of God as mystery and as the mystery which presents itself as the source of forgiveness, salvation and eternal life. In eternity our vision of God will be clearer but it will still contain an element of mystery.

We come to whatever knowledge is possible about God when we understand knowledge

---

[13] All the Rahner quotations in this chapter are taken from 'The Hiddenness of God' in *Theological Investigations*, Vol. 16.

[14] M. Buber, *I and Thou*, (Edinburgh: T & T Clark 1937) 168. Hereafter *I and Thou*.

not only as comprehending something, but also as an openness to mystery - to the mystery of the Being who is incomprehensible. Rahner says: 'Knowledge in this primary sense is the presence of the mystery itself. It is being addressed by what no longer has a name, and it is relying on a reality which is not mastered but is itself the master. It is the speech of a being without a name, about which clear statements are impossible; it is the last moment before the dumbness which is needed if the silence is to be heard, and God is to be worshipped in love... It's silent presence can be ignored in the face of immediate phenomena which in their variety and particularity can fill the space of life and consciousness'.

Simone Weil, the French philospher, says that distraction is the root of sin. By this she means that the world is given to distraction because we can so easily get caught up in external pheonomena rather than face living at the deeper level of the spirit, of mystery.

This openness to mystery can be experienced even if not known; it is a reaching beyond the conceptual to the nameless, the incomprehensible. Our transcendence allows for this possibility and when touched by grace it becomes actual. It is an experience of overwhelming mystery - the mystery that is both origin and goal of all that is. The only response is to surrender to the mystery of the incomprehensibility of God.

J e s u s

Jesus stands like us as a human being in faith before Absolute Mystery. Rahner spells this out as follows: 'He surrendered himself unconditionally in his mind to the incomprehensibility of God and accepted with love this "blessed ignorance"... This ignorance of Jesus, for which there is ample evidence in Scripture, does not point to a deficiency, but rather to a positive merit in his acceptance of this ignorance.' Paul, using a possible liturgical formula, says: 'He emptied himself to assume the condition of a slave, and became as men are' (Phil 2:7). Jesus could not empty himself of his divinity but he chose not to allow his divine knowledge penetrate his human consciousness.

How we talk about Jesus being God is difficult. It is essentially an experiential knowing in the sense that Christians experience Jesus doing what God does, namely, saving, giving life, ruling us, being our master. It is our experience of Jesus that tells us he is God. How we make this intelligible to others is the problem.

How do we approach/ enter Absolute Mystery?

Believing, hoping, loving, the three theological virtues, are the means by which we make contact with God. The role of faith, hope, and charity, is to draw us towards God. To believe, to hope, to love, is to encounter God.

Our presence to absolute mystery is not founded on feelings. A feeling of dryness does not prove God's absence. A feeling of warmth does not prove God's presence. John of the Cross, the well-known mystical writer says: 'Phenomena, visions, inner words in themselves cannot help one in the love of God as much as the smallest act of living faith and hope.' We live in a culture which delights in the extraordinary. But humility, self-emptying, simplicity, silence are the dispositions that make room for us to receive God.

Absolute Mystery Revealed to us as Trinity of Persons

As Christians we speak about God as Trinity. Jesus brought us the great revelation that God's inner life was Trinitarian. 'The Trinity sums up the mystery of who God is'.[15] Being a Christian is essentially about making the Trinity real in our lives and then living out of that reality. Even though the Trinitarian mystery is something to be lived people seem to make very little use of it in their Christian lives. Rahner and Balthasar observed that most Christians are in practice strict monotheists, namely, they believe in a monopersonal God. Generally speaking the church in its teaching speaks largely of a personal God instead of the full truth - a tripersonal God.

---

[15] This quotation and many of the ideas in this section are drawn from W. Kasper, *The God of Jesus Christ* (London: SCM Press 1982). Present quotation p.268. Hereafter *The God of Jesus Christ*. Walter Kasper is a German theologian.

Our knowledge of Trinity comes through revelation - the historical self-revelation of the Father, through Jesus Christ in the Holy Spirit. But even after the revelation of the Trinity by Jesus the Trinity remains mystery. God is only revealed to us through the medium of history and through human words and deeds, namely, in finite forms. God is known indirectly through his effects. These effects become their clearest in Jesus - he is the essential symbol of who God is. He leads us into the Mystery of God which he reveals to us precisely as mystery.

Many Old Testament passages prepare for this definitive Trinitarian revelation while at the same time leaving an incomplete picture:
1. The book of Genesis depicts God speaking in the plural. 'Let us make man in our image' (1:26).
2. In the Mamre scene we see three heavenly visitors visiting Abraham. (see Gen 18:1-15).
3. The 'Angel of God' is a revelatory figure who is shown sometimes as distinct from God, while at other times the figure is identical with God. This 'angel of the Lord' is a symbol to bridge the gap between the being of God who is incomprehensible to us and God's presence active in history.
4. Later writings hint at certain personifications in God, for example, divine wisdom, divine word, divine spirit. All these personifications point to a wealth of life within the Godhead.

In the New Testament Jesus reveals to us the mystery of the Trinity.
John's gospel for instance has Jesus saying 'To have seen me is to have seen the Father' (1:9) and 'The Father and I are one' (10:29).
Paul says 'I proclaim Jesus Christ, the revelation of a mystery kept secret for endless ages' (Rm 16:26).

The definitive revelation that 'God is love' (1 Jn 4:16) is spelt out by the Trinity of Persons. The Son of God is the Thou of the Father, and the love between them is the Spirit. In the Spirit we are caught up into the communion of love that exists between all three persons.

The Unity of God

While there is a Trinity of persons in God there is also unity. The unity within God is a oneness of identity which can be termed Godness. Unity presupposes multiplicity in the sense that oneness implies there are two or more other 'things'. For example, because there is one food category known as vegetables we can then speak of two or three types of vegetables, just as we can say two or three people since there is one human nature.

A question arises: is there an overall unity that embraces all of reality? If there were no all-embracing unity that took in all reality everything would be random and lack order and meaning. Polytheism coped with this problem by naming a supreme God; Buddhists and Hindus maintain all reality is a single unity.

Throughout the Old Testament Yahweh is seen as one God and superior to all others. Monotheism in the Old Testament is not a philosophical question but the fruit of religious experience. They knew that unconditional trustworthiness is to be found in God alone.

The distinguishing element in Christianity is this: that the ultimate ground of the unity and wholeness of reality is not a scheme, a structure, a principle, but is personal: one God in three persons. This is the answer to the primordial question of humanity. Kasper in his work with the striking title 'The God of Jesus Christ' refers to a unity that does not absorb multiplicity but turns it into a unified whole, a unity that is not impoverishment, but fullness and completion. The oneness of God means unqualified uniqueness. If there were two Gods then one would limit the other, cause fragmentation even if there were interpenetration. Anything else that is absolutized, a person, thing, idea, the devil, is a false God and therefore an idol.

According to Leftow there are no separate centres of consciousness and decision-making within the Godhead.[16] The differentiation within God, namely the distinction of persons as understood by Christianity, does not do away with the oneness of God but rather makes it

---

[16] B. Leftow, refered to by G. O'Collins, 'Grappling with the Trinity' in *The Tablet* 9 May 1998.

meaningful. Trinity is Christianity's concrete expression of monotheism; the living God means a triune God. Holding together Trinity and Unity lies at the heart of the mystery of God - a mystery we grapple with but above all enter in a spirit of humble love.

The Trinity is the Mystery of the Christian Faith

The Trinity is a mystery of inexhaustible richness. The mystery of the Trinity is also the deepest ground and meaning of the mystery of the human person and of the latter's fulfilment in love. The vital core, energy, sustaining force, within the inner Trinitarian life is intimate relationships. Relationships are also vital to full human living. Our likeness to God, since we are made in God's image, is seen most clearly in our ability to relate to others and to the Other.

In God not only the unity but also the distinction, in this case of persons and their roles, is always greater than in the created world. The distinction is relational - the Father is not the Son, the Son is not the Father and neither are the Spirit. In God there is the twofold dynamic of being-from-another and being-for-another. The different properties or activities in the Trinity, while common to all persons are appropriated to a particular person, for example, power to the Father, wisdom to the Son and love to the Spirit.

When modern philosophers and psychologists use the term 'person' the notion of relation is strongly to the fore. In other words central to the modern understanding of person is that we only exist in relationship: I-Thou-We. In the light of this understanding an isolated unipersonal God would be less meaningful today as an explanation of who God is - a fact which re-enforces further our need to make the Trinity a living reality in our lives.

Any analogy between ourselves and God is always more dissimilar than similar so the rich interrelational life of the Trinity is far beyond what we can imagine. If we are dialogical beings so is the Trinity, only more so. They are dialogue. The Father is pure self enunciation, namely he speaks/expresses his whole self in the person of the Son, the Word; the Son is pure hearing and heeding of the Father; the Holy Spirit is pure reception, pure gift'.[17]

God the Father - Abba

An 'I' without a 'Thou' is an impoverishment and is therefore an impossibility in God. Humanity cannot be God's 'Thou' since this is a relationship of inequality.[18] The mystery of the Trinity is the mystery of the necessity of the Thou for the I.

Our faith ultimately stands not on belief in Jesus but on belief in the 'God of Jesus Christ'. Jesus refers to God as 'Abba Father'. He also refers to his Father as 'My Father and Your Father', 'Your Father in Heaven'. Jesus reveals God as Father not only in words but in deed by the actions of his entire life.

Gospels

The first half of John's gospel, chapters 1-12, has one theme: Jesus' relationship with the Father. The second half is concerned with the sending of the Spirit whose role is to recall and make present the work of Jesus.

Epistles

Paul in many of his letters uses the phrase 'the Father of our Lord Jesus Christ' (e.g. Eph 1:3; Col 1:4). He also refers to the Father as 'a gentle Father and the God of all consolation who comforts us in all our sorrows so that we can offer others, in their sorrows, the consolation we have received from God ourselves' (2 Cor 1:3-4). James refers to the Father as the source of life and light: 'All that is good, everything that is perfect, which is give us from above; it comes down from the Father of all Light' (James 1:17).

The Creed

The creed starts with the Father as 'the summit of unity'. One could say divinity originates in

---

[17] *The God of Jesus Christ*, 290.

[18] The divine-human relationship has the potential to be one of extraordinary intimacy yet it can never be a relationship of equality since we are created beings and God is uncreated being. Using imagery we can say that the very real spark set alight in the human-divine relationship relationship can never become the full fire.

the Father and streams forth in the Son and Holy Spirit; or, the Father acts through the Son in the Holy Spirit. 'He who sees me sees the Father' (Jn 14:9); in other words the absolute incomprehensible nature of the Father is made comprehensible in Jesus.

In this Abba relationship our own filial relationship is disclosed. The Resurrection is a manifestation of the power of the Father that is ascribed to the action of the Spirit. Since that event, not only Jesus but we too are empowered to participate in this powerful life of the Spirit; it is through the Spirit that we can cry out 'Abba, Father' (Rm 8:15).

Summary

In summary we could say the Trinity is concerned with the self-communication of God both within the inter-Trinitarian life as well as in the Trinity's relation to creation. The Trinity essentially says that the one God is not a solitary God. To say that God is solitary is to fall into the heresy of theism.

Only because God is overflowing love within his very being can he allow that love to overflow freely in his initial and on-going work of creating. Only because God is love in himself can he be love for us. This love is not marked by a need to give, but rather is a love that gives out of its own overflowing fullness - it is a self-outpouring: 'In the Father love exists as pure source that pours itself out; in the Son it exists as pure passing-on, as pure mediation; in the Spirit it exists as the joy of pure receiving'.[19]

The selflessness of love lies at the heart of that mystery since 'the Trinitarian persons are characterized by their selflessness. They are each in their own way pure surrender. Their eternal kenotic existence is the condition for the possibility of the temporal kenosis/self-emptying of the Son, and thus a type of Christian humility and selfless service'.[20]

The challenge to atheism today is not a feeble, vague, watered-down theism but a decisive

---

[19] Ibid. 308.
[20] Ibid. 310.

witness to the living God of history who has disclosed himself in a concrete way through Jesus Christ in the Holy Spirit. The proclamation of the triune God is of the greatest pastoral importance today. It is the acknowledgement of the Godness of God that leads to the humanization of man. The proclamation of the death of God leads to the proclamation of the death of man.

The above explanation is not intended as an intellectual exercise but rather is an attempt at a faith-filled understanding of the Trinitarian mystery as mystery. A 'Trinity Summit' was held in New York in Easter week 1998. G. O'Collins, who reported on the summit, noted participants remarks that faith in the Trinity provided 'only background music for many of their fellow Christians' and that 'the scholars at the summit hoped to encourage a full Trinitarian focus in life and worship. For too long, belief in the Trinity has been seen as a logical puzzle for experts rather than a vibrant doctrine to live and die for'.[21]

The scholars grappled with the perennial challenge of how to save the threeness of God and not lose the divine unity. They pointed out the Trinity cannot be reduced to the model of a loving family or a united committee since human comparisons always fall short. From the pastoral perspective it was stated that in a survey of 3,500 sermons only twenty reflected on the Trinity.

Reflection

- Allow the amazingness of the mystery of God to enfold you, to penetrate your deepest self.

- Read reflectively some verses of Jesus' prayer to his Father in John 17.

---

[21] G. O'Collins, 'Grappling with the Trinity' in *The Tablet* 9th May 1998.

The Holy Spirit

S c u l p t u r e

Ken Thompson gives the following description of his work. 'The Holy Spirit, we are told, is not seen, only his effect is felt. Hence the negative as he passes through the stone! My stone carving of the Holy Spirit symbolised by a dove, demonstrates that it is the result of His actions that the Third Person of the Holy Trinity is recognized. Like the invisible wind's effect on matter, the Holy Spirit's effect is found mysteriously in our personal lives and human history. My sculpture is the imaginary result of the passage of a dove through stone; pleasing, I hope, not only to the mind but also to the eye'.

This sculpture is deliberately placed near water, at the edge of the waterfall which divides the upper from the lower pond. 'God's spirit hovered over the water' (Gn.1:2) as God sets out on his work of creating. The same Spirit is continuously present in the on-going work of creation - in the universe and within ourselves. While this is the smallest piece in the collection the outline of the dove between the two ponds is striking. This is the only piece too that is made from a synthetic material - reconstituted stone. This fact, like the image of the negative, highlights the imperceptibility of the Spirit's presence in all of creation. The fan-shape of the overall piece suggests expansiveness, being opened out - realities that are linked with the Holy Spirit's role.

This reflection on the Spirit has three sub-sections titled: The Biblical Symbols of the Spirit, The Holy Spirit Makes our Experience of God Possible, The Holy Spirit is Known by His Effects.

B i b l i c a l   S y m b o l s   o f   t h e   S p i r i t

D o v e

The dove is the most concrete biblical symbol of the Spirit. In the opening sentence of the bible the action of 'hovering over the water' (Gn 1:1) suggests a bird. The fluttering of wings creates a movement of air suggesting a generation of energy - the force which initiates God's creative work. This image of energy at the beginning of creation links well with the big bang theory. An analogy can also be made between the creation story and scientists who say that a butterfly fluttering its wings in one part of the world can be the initial generation of energy that can set in motion a movement of air that finally becomes a hurricane on the opposite side of the globe.

Other more specific references to a dove are found in the Psalms, the Song of Songs and Isaiah. For example: 'O for the wings of a dove to fly away and find rest' (Ps 55.6).

The most significant text is the presence of the Spirit manifested as a dove at Jesus' baptism: 'I saw the spirit coming down on him from heaven like a dove and resting on him' (Jn 1:33).

The word 'Father' and 'Son' are metaphors and so too is the word 'Spirit'. The elemental word-symbols of air, fire and water are powerful symbols of the Spirit. Each of these symbols convey to us something about the Spirit's person, presence and role.

Air - Breath, Ruah

Ruah is the Hebrew word for both breath and spirit. The Spirit is seen not merely as the source of life but as the source of an individual personality.

In the second creation story earth and Spirit are the essential elements that make us human: 'God fashioned man of dust from the soil. Then he breathed into his nostrils a breath of life, and thus *Adamah* became a living being' (Gn 2:7). The energy that God releases by His own breath creates the human person. He does not create from some force outside himself but from the depth of his own being, namely, his own Spirit. Holy Breath, or Divine Breath are thus apt titles for the Holy Spirit.

In the on-going work of creation the Spirit creates by operating from within creation; from within the processes that make up our created world and its history. The Spirit acts from

within our spirit; her action is operative in our desires, our love, our freedom. Freedom of choice is God's gift to man. God never takes back his gifts and so he never compels or forces us in the choices we make. When we respond with love and goodness the Spirit is active in that response.

The Spirit's essential activity is one which inspires, urges us to love, to love the good and especially to love each other. We have the freedom to follow or not follow this inspiration. The Spirit is present in all the major and minor happenings of the universe and this includes the happenings of our personal lives whether we are aware of this or not.

Old Testament examples of moments when the Spirit's presence became manifest under the symbol of wind or breath are:
'Come from the four winds: breath; breathe on these dead; let them live....I shall put my spirit in you, and you will live' (Ez 37:9).
'The Lord was not in the mighty wind, the earthquake or the fire but in the gentle breeze' (1 Kg 20:12).
New Testament examples include:
'The wind blows wherever it pleases; you hear its sound but you cannot tell where it comes from or where it is going. That is how it is with all who are born of the spirit' (Jn 3:7).
'Bowing his head he gave up his spirit' (Jn 19:30). The last breath of Jesus is a symbol of the outpouring of the Spirit on all humankind.
'He breathed on them and said: 'Receive the Holy Spirit. For those whose sins you forgive they are forgiven...' (Jn 20:22).
'Suddenly they heard what sounded like a powerful wind from heaven the noise of which filled the entire house in which they were sitting' (Acts 2:1).

The symbol of air in the form of wind as a sign of the Spirit's presence evokes an awareness of the omnipresent nature of that presence. Wind power is a source of energy, so too is the Spirit. Love is the energising force in interpersonal relating and the Spirit is the bond of love that unites all things. But the release of this energy of the Spirit is, like wind unpredictable.

Jesus tells us: 'The wind blows where it pleases...you cannot tell where it comes from or where it is going. So it is with everyone born of the Spirit' (Jn 3:8). A key sign of the release of that Spirit-energy is empowerment in those who receive it.

Fire

Fire is a strong symbol of the divine presence. In the Old Testament for instance the fire manifested in the pillar of fire and the burning bush were two clear signs of God's presence. In the New Testament we see fire as a clear sign of the coming of the Spirit at Pentecost. 'Something appeared to them that seemed like tongues of fire, these separated and came to rest on the head of each of them. They were all filled with the Holy Spirit' (Acts 2:1). Jesus made references to fire as the following passages show: 'He will baptise you with the Holy Spirit and fire' (Lk 3:16); 'I have come to bring fire to the earth and how I wish it were blazing already' (Lk 12:49).

Water

There are hints of water's association with the spirit in the Old Testament, for example, 'I shall pour clean water over you and you will be cleansed.. I shall give you a new heart and put a new spirit in you...I shall put my spirit in you' (Ez 36:25).

There are several New Testament texts which link water with the Holy Spirit:

- 'Unless a man is born through water and the Spirit he cannot enter the kingdom of God' (Jn 3:5).
- 'Anyone who drinks the water that I shall give [living water] will never be thirsty again: the water I shall give will turn into a spring inside him, welling up to eternal life' (Jn 4:14).
- 'If any man is thirsty, let him come to me! Let the man come and drink who believes in me! As scripture says: From his breast shall flow fountains of living water. He was speaking of the Spirit which those who believed in him were to receive; for there was no spirit as yet because Jesus had not yet been glorified' (Jn 7:38).

The Holy Spirit Makes Our Experience of God Possible

A fundamental question is: how is it possible for us to experience the Divine in our lives? Love is the core of our experience of God. To be in love is to be in love with someone and at the heart of all love is self-surrender to another person. The person we surrender to is the Spirit - that gift of God which God offers us; a spring which wells up from deep within us. (See Jn 4:10,14). It is through that Spirit that we experience, encounter God.

The inner Trinitarian life is constituted by the varying relationships of self-surrender that causes each of the three persons to be:

The Father becomes Father in the self-surrendering love whereby He expresses himself in the Word - the Son. The Father as pure self-giving love cannot exist without the Son.

The Son not only reciprocates this love by receiving the gift of Sonship for himself but gives himself back to the Father. (See Jesus' priestly prayer in Jn 17). The Son is therefore pure gratitude, eternal Eucharist.

The intensity of this bond of loving surrender between the Father and Son extends beyond itself. It is pure giving which empties itself, gives-away this two-in-oneness which results in a third person - the *Holy Spirit* in whom this love exists as pure receiving.

This *self-surrendering action of God* [or self-emptying process] is manifested in God's relationship with us. God - Abba, so loved us that he gave us his Son... The Son showed how perfect his love was by giving up his life and by so doing gave us his Spirit.

This important dimension of self-surrender within human existence expresses itself in being-open-to-receive this Spirit of unrestricted love into our hearts. 'The love of God has been poured into our hearts by the Holy Spirit which has been given us' (Rm 5:5). The Spirit when received becomes the inward principle of our lives, the undertow of our existence. The only response is to let be what is. This letting-be is not something passive but involves the active acceptance of cooperating with the Spirit. Such cooperation allows the Spirit to become the core principle which colours the formation of our attitudes and which provides the loving energy for our actions. This is what faith is; it is saying an explicit 'yes' to the Spirit's presence and action in our lives.

Because God is love 'he is able to empty himself out in history and in this very emptying reveal his glory. Because God in himself is pure gift, he is able to give himself in the Holy Spirit. As the innermost being of God, the Spirit is at the same time the outermost, the condition for the possibility of creation and redemption. ...Just as he is God's way to what is outside himself so also he effects the return of all created reality to God'.[22] The Pentecost sequence describes the Spirit as 'the finger of God's right hand'. This image depicts the Spirit as the furthest outreach of God.

How does this experience come about?

Our experience of God is not the result of our personal knowledge or choice. No one can decide or reason themselves into falling in love. Ordinarily knowledge precedes love. The experience of falling in love is the exception to love preceding knowledge.

A *minor exception* is when two people fall in love. It is an experience, according to Lonergan, of something disproportionate to its 'causes, conditions, occasions, antecedents.'[23] It results in our whole world changing, undergoing a new organization. It is like a new beginning. Knowledge of the other person increases over time after the initial event. That knowledge is illuminated by the love that preceded it as well as the love that continues to be its source and foundation.

The *major exception* concerns the human divine relationship. When *God's love floods our heart* we are exposed to an unmediated experience of mystery which cannot be named or explained. The experience is mysterious, especially in the early stages, since 'who it is we love is neither given nor as yet understood'.[24] This experience will vary in intensity from person to person and resonate differently according to people's temperaments. It is an experience of

[22] *The God of Jesus Christ* 311.
[23] *Method* 122.
[24] Ibid.

immediacy where thoughts, words, symbols lose their relevance and even disappear.

A consequence of this experience is that the love of God transforms our knowledge and our values. It 'takes over' our ways of thinking and acting. From the beginning it is a conscious experience.[25] 'Because the dynamic state [of being in love with God] is conscious without being known, it is an experience of mystery. Because it is being in love, the mystery is not merely attractive but fascinating; to it one belongs; by it one is possessed'.[26] P.Tillich[27] speaks of it as an experience of being grasped by ultimate concern.

In human love lovers, after the initial experience of falling in love, only get to know each other by revealing their love to each other by outward expressions such as words, gestures and deeds. Without outward forms of expression love would not reach the point of full surrender of one person to the other.

So too it is by word, the word of religion, that that prior inner word or immediate experience of God flooding our hearts becomes better known. In other words religion helps us to put words on, articulate our inner experience.[28] We need the outer word to help us to come to know and live out that primary experience of the Spirit's presence within our lives. This outer word manifests itself through language or symbol. For Christians - the greatest outward expression of that prior inner word comes to us in the Word Incarnate - Jesus.

In the post Pentecost era we have a threefold word that enables us to hear the Jesus word, namely, the word of the gospel, the word of community, and the word of tradition. All three help us realise that God first loved us.

---

[25] Consciousness is just experience. Knowledge on the other hand is a combination of experience, understanding and judging.

[26] Ibid. 106.

[27] Paul Tillich is a German theologian.

[28] Normally that inner word finds expression in the religious cultural context of the individual. It could be Budhist, Jewish, Christian. It is at this level of primary religious experience that inter-faith dialogue is more likely to prove fruitful since this core experience is for all faiths a source of unity. People who live in non-religious cultures, such as is found in countries of Europe today, will find it more difficult to articulate and give outward expression to this primary inner experience of the Divine in their lives.

The primary experience of the inner word, the Spirit's presence in our lives, occurs on the fourth level of human consciousness - that area that makes judgements of value. When we are in love, and in this instance in love with God, this love does not initially require understanding and truth judgements, since the inner experience itself reveals values we had not appreciated before, values like repentance, forgiveness, self-sacrificing love, worship. However as we are assisted more and more by the outer word to articulate and elaborate on our inner experience we come to fuller truth. That mediated truth propels us to make choices that lead to responsible action - action that benefits ourselves and the rest of humanity.

Religious conversion or falling in love with God is essentially a response, a saying 'yes', which allows the gift of God's love to occupy the ground of our fourth level of consciousness - that part of our consciousness where we make the choices about how we live our lives. This falling in love, saying 'yes' to God, is the essential note that makes us believers.

As a person reflects on this experience there is a wanting to know more who God is as well as how we can integrate this experience more consistently with the rest of our lives. To do this the first three stages of consciousness - experiencing, understanding and judging are brought into play.

We have seen that our ability to question reveals we are transcendent beings, namely, we constantly search for the more of truth, for what lies beyond our present horizon. Our ability to receive God's love, especially when it becomes a state of being in love with Unrestricted Love, is the fulfilment of our capacity for self-transcendence. To be in love without conditions is to be in love with someone transcendent. When that Transcendent Person is God, God becomes real to us from within. When we respond by loving that Transcendent Other - God - we transcend ourselves.

True loving demands loving attention to the other and when this other is God we call this loving attention prayer. Loving also involves loving all that the Beloved loves so this means loving all God's people and the whole of creation.

The Holy Spirit is Known by His Effects

The religious experience described above manifests itself in changed attitudes and behaviour which are listed in scripture under the fruits of the Spirit - love, joy, kindness, goodness, fidelity, gentleness and self-control. (See Gal 5:22).

Lonergan spells this out as follows: 'Being in love with God is the basic fulfilment... that brings *a deep-set joy* that can remain despite humiliation, failure, privation, pain, betrayal, desertion. That fulfilment brings a *radical peace*, the peace that the world cannot give. That fulfilment bears fruit in a *love of one's neighbour* that strives mightily to bring about the kingdom of God on earth. On the other hand, the absence of that fulfilment opens the way to the trivialisation of human life in the pursuit of fun, to the harshness of human life arising from the ruthless exercise of power, to despair about human welfare springing from the conviction that the universe is absurd.'[29]

Simone Weil points out that the only power God has in relation to human beings, whom he gifted with free will, is the power that inspires us to love. Compulsion is foreign to love. Freedom to say 'yes' or 'no' to God is inherant to the divine/human relationship. Freedom is also vital in all human relationships. Love is power and is the only force we can use that leaves people dignified and free. That power of love, expressed in freedom, is implanted deep within us through the gift of the Holy Spirit. We cannot reach out to others without that power becoming operative. We certainly cannot reach out to God without the Spirit's help. 'It is the Spirit that makes it possible for us to say 'Abba, Father' (Rm 8:16).

Recognizing and Growing in Our Life in the Spirit

Personal experience of the Spirit varies from person to person. Rarely is the event sudden. The state of being in love with God is often preceded by moments of love which predispose towards the state of being in love. But once a certain state of being in love is established this requires to be filled out and developed as with any loving human relationship. The life of the

---

[29] Ibid 105.

Spirit begins with listening to the voice that lies deep within our own spirit. The Spirit is also experienced when we listen to our own limitless longing to love and be loved. Developing the life of the Spirit in our lives flows from keeping in touch with our deep-down longings, from asking searching questions, and from expanding and deepening our loving.

However, our ability to self-transcend, namely to accept the love of another, and in this instance the Spirit of love, always remains precarious. Lonergan points out there is always tension between the self in the process of transcending and the self as transcended. To be a fully transcended person, namely a completely authentic human being is a goal. We are never in full possession of this. We have to fight against our own selfishness, between being authentic or inauthentic as we journey on the road of self-transcendence. This entails living our lives more and more for the Other and for others.

Reflection

Ponder:
- The gift of God, namely the person of the Spirit, that dwells intimately within you: 'The love of God has been poured into our hearts by the Holy Spirit which has been given us' (Rm 5:5).

- How this loving Presence of the Spirit is available to you to motivate and empower you in all you do.

- Your ability to surrender yourself to this empowerment of the Spirit. This entails being less bound by the restrictive limits of your own thinking and loving and more open to the action of the Spirit in you.

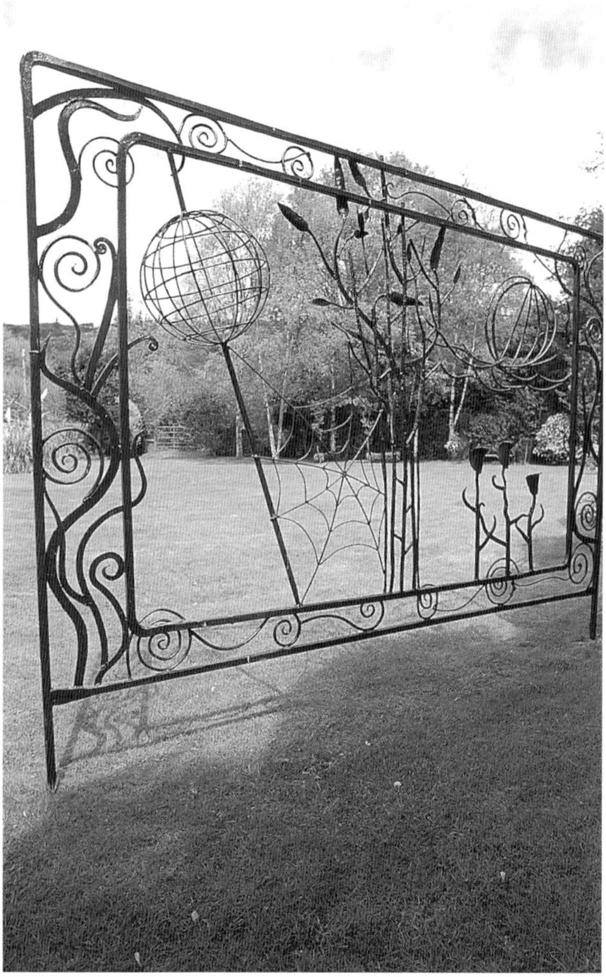

Creation of the Universe

Sculpture

Paul Pages's four metal frames form the basis for this reflection on the whole of creation. Each frame depicts various items mentioned in the biblical creation story like the sun, moon, stars, the earth, and other biblical nature images such as lightening, rain, cloud and rainbow, as well as the elements fire and water. Each frame is set in a celtic frieze acting as a reminder that we live in Ireland in the celtic part of the universe's planet Earth.[30]

Overview

The Bible uses many symbolic images, especially those of the universe, to express truths about God and his creative activity. As salvation history unfolds these truths became clearer. The exploration of truth continues in present day salvation history. We need to decipher, to grow in understanding about what the images, symbols, stories and in general what the great use of the imagination in the Bible is saying about truth and the meaning of our existence. We also need to use our own gifts of imagination in finding some relevant new images and symbols that will reveal God's truth in greater clarity to the modern believer and unbeliever.

A biblical approach to discern meaning differs from a scientific one. Neither approach contradicts the other but rather both together further our attempts to answer ultimate questions.

- *Scientific truth* offers factual truths about concrete reality but these answers on their own fail to satisfy the human heart on the profounder questions concerning existence. The universe, according to scientists, came into being with the big bang theory fifteen billion years ago.
- *Biblical truth* centres on the deep desires of the human spirit for truth, beauty, love and freedom. Such truth can only be discovered by moving beyond the realm of science.

The miracle of the big bang is the fact that in the first few milliseconds that followed this

---

[30] The illustration shows only one of these four frames.

explosion conditions were put in place from which the universe, and at a later stage life on earth, and then finally ourselves came to be. Who was responsible for this miracle? Why did it come about? It is the philosophers and religious people who try to fathom these 'who' and 'why' questions.

If we are to feel comfortable, at home in the universe and not experience it as a hostile place we need to discover or re-discover that at the centre of it's origin, it's on-going creation, as well as it's destiny, is a loving heart - God. Just as God is mystery and the human person is mystery, so too the universe is profoundly mysterious.

The idea of creation existed in Near Eastern cultures for example in Egypt and Mesopotamia before the time of Abraham but it was bound up by polytheistic ideas or many Gods.

The outline of this reflection follows the Genesis creation story. The various creation events mentioned in this story, and especially the ones depicted in this sculpture, are particularly noted and their symbolic value highlighted.

Biblical Revelation

We need to heighten our awareness of our personal sense of history regarding not only the evolution of the physical world but also humanity's development in thought and this includes the biblical understanding of God. We learn through history. A lack of a sense of history, coupled with the present day culture of 'the instant', be it, for example, coffee or the compulsion for immediate satisfaction, leads to an impoverished understanding of ideas and how they have come to be what they are in our particular culture and age. It is through our idea of reality that we arrive at personal meaning.

To grow in a truer perception of reality necessitates we go back and trace how our present thinking has come to be what it is today. There is need also to stay open to the future as present history unfolds. There is great truth in the cliche: 'To give people back a past is to give people back a future'. Rahner says that when we neglect history we become 'inhuman and disorientated'.

The Hebrew/Christian understanding of creation evolved. It is summed up in its most intense form in the revelation of God's name: Yahweh, which means 'He who brings to be'. In other words Yahweh is a creator God.

Abraham period

Melchizideck blesses Abraham 'by God the most high who created heaven and earth' (Gn 14:19). Abraham himself takes as his witness 'God most high, who created heaven and earth'. It took the powerful historical figure of Abraham to make the breakthrough of realizing both the *oneness of God* and that God was the *creator of everything*. Israelite faith was always monotheistic, but in their early history they accepted other people having more than one God. Only during the exile period (600 B.C. approximately) they came to an understanding that 'I am one God and beside me there is no other'.

Genesis 1

This first, although later creation story than the one found in Genesis 2 uses a majestic format. The core issue in the story is that creation is the result of God's personal activity. God draws the created world out of *primeval chaos* and brings forth beauty, richness, life. The author is struck by the order of everything. He states strongly that everything created is put in place by the *power of God's word* (Ps 148:5). There is no sign of monsters, demons or a struggle as with other mythologies, such as the Babylonians. God acts alone, spontaneously and according to his plan. This plan focuses on the human person for whose sake the created world exists.

This text gives us a story that uses the literary form of myth to express it's truth. The story does not clash with modern evolutionary theories. The numbers in this story, namely, the days of the week, are symbolic. The fact that the world as we know it took billions of years to come to its present state of existence does not take in the least from the truth that 'through him all things came to be, not one thing had its being but through him' (Jn 1:2).

Other post-exile writings

The books of Proverbs and Wisdom reveal that wisdom is personified and is the craftsman of creation (see Wis 8:6, 9:9; Pv 8:22-31). God gives glimpses of himself through all his created works (see Wis 13:1-5).

On-going creation.

The Genesis story gives us the starting point for the plan of God and the history of salvation. Clearly everything that happens from then on is also dependent on God - all happenings, world history, my personal history. 'It was you who created by inmost self, and put me together in my mother's womb' (Ps 139:13). The hairs on our head, our thoughts and feelings, all lie within God's creation. Put in reverse: nothing lies outside God.

There are significant moments in biblical history which reveal God's ongoing creative work. Highly important is the notion of election - being specially chosen by God. The Israelites became aware they were specially chosen as a people and this fact was made known to them through key moments in their history. For example: the special covenant with Abraham and his descendants and with Moses and the Israelite nation. The new covenant offered through Christ to the new People of God, his church was also a sign of election. The understanding of what this election means has changed over history. For instance, the Catholic understanding of church since Vatican 11 is that the church 'embraces', 'is in solidarity with', the whole human family. It is worth noting too, that Sinai and Pentecost, the two key moments where the covenant initially given to Abraham was ratified, were community events.

The created universe strains towards fulfilment

where the paradise of the new Jerusalem offers a new order that will last forever. The whole universe will share in this new transformation of 'a new heaven and a new earth' (Is 65:17,18. Rev. 21:1).

THE EARTH

In the beginning of the Old Testament in Genesis 1:1 God first creates heaven and earth. 'In the beginning God created the heavens and the earth'. Earth at this stage is a 'formless void'

or *tohu* in Hebrew. The meaning of this word is uncertain but it expresses something like waste, emptiness, darkness. It is clear however that the term from the author's perspective was a symbol of chaos. After the exile and at the time of Paul there is the realization that the tohu word-symbol offers an image of nothingness; that God existed before creation and that he created out of nothing. Nothingness is a speculative concept. The bible's mythological description of the creation is a powerful way of leading us to the truth of the story of creation.

This primal 2,500 year old biblical imagery is replaced by today's scientific view of a mass of gas which led to the big bang. The actual image or theory used is secondary. The fact that created being came into existence is astonishing. It is a cause for immense wonder. A deepening awareness that only the power of Being/ the totally Transcendent Other/ the Uncreated One/ which we name God, and a God which we know by revelation to be personal, calls for adoration and gratitude.

God lets dry land appear as he collects the water together in one 'place'- the 'seas' (v.9-12). On this same 'third day' is included creating the earth to be fruitful. It is to produce vegetation: seeds, plants, trees, fruits. It would in other words be self-perpetuating, the fruits producing the seed; the seeds producing fruits.

The earth in the sense of 'the land' plays an important role in the history of salvation. It is crucial still today in modern Israel as seen by the importance of 'the territories'.God's opening invitation and promise to Abraham, the beginning of factual biblical history, is to 'Come to the land that I will show you..for I mean to give it to you' (Gn 12:1). This gift of the land in which they are to settle was a sign of God's blessing. Yet the land was often taken away from them by conquest leading to the Israelites being exiled in a foreign country. Such periods were seen as times of purification to make them realize their ultimate dependency was to be on God, not on land.

At the close of the twentieth century we realize it is not just our patch that is important, though there still remains the call to be a good steward and to beautify our 'spot'. Now we see we are responsible for the good of the whole earth in some way. There is a new cosmic/global consciousness emerging of which the green movements are a manifestation.

Jesus

Like us, Jesus was earthbound. His imagination was formed by the images of his country. He was shaped by its landscape, climate. He uses many earth images in his teaching - sheep, weather, harvest, wine etc. 'He was bound to the land of Israel by all the fibres of his being'.[31] Ultimately he chose bread and wine, the fruit of the earth, as the symbols through which he leaves us his real Eucharistic presence throughout the remainder of time.

The *Celtic freeze* portrayed in the sculpture reminds us that like Jesus we are shaped by our native Celtic culture which grew out of the landscape of Ireland. Celtic art has many symbols but is particularly characterised by its flowing and intertwining spirals and circles. J. O'Donohue says: 'The Celtic mind was ever drawn to the single line; it avoided ways of seeing and being which seek satisfaction in certainty. The Celtic mind had a wonderful respect for the mystery of the circle and the spiral. The circle is one of the oldest and most powerful symbols. The world is a circle; the sun and moon are too. Even time itself has a circular nature... The circle embraces depth and height together. The circle never reduces the mystery to a single direction or preference.. Our imagination follows the rhythm of the circle'.[32]

Our vision is thus not linear. The linear, the shortest route timewise, can seem the most efficient but it is not necessarily the most effective since it can miss things. The curved path is often more beautiful. It also facilitates meandering which allows us greater time to ponder, to stand and stare. 'Perception is crucial to understanding. How you see and what you see determines how you will be. Your perception, or your view of reality is the lens through which you see things. For example, we tend to perceive difficulty as disturbance. Ironically difficulty can be a great friend of creativity...'[33]

---

[31] L. Dufour, ed., *Dictionary of Biblical Theology* (London: Geoffrey Chapman 1970). 108.
[32] J. O'Donohue, *Anam Cara* (London: Bantam Press 1997). 108. Hereafter *Anam Cara*. John O'Donohue is an Irish philosophical theologian.
[33] Ibid 193.

LIGHT - SUN, MOON, STARS

God's first formal act of creation following that of the earth itself was light. (v.3-5). The names of the sun and moon are deliberately omitted in this creation story because both were deified by neighbouring nations. Instead there is reference to 'the greater light' -the sun; and 'the lesser light' - the moon and the stars. All are situated in the 'vault of heaven'. Their purpose is to shine on/illuminate the earth. (v.14-19).

With the creation of light came the creation of time. The light/darkness cycle of the earth's rotation around the sun becomes the measure of one day; the lunar movements dictate the span of our months and years.

The *light/darkness theme* is significant in the Old Testament but it takes on a new centrality in the New Testament where Jesus claims in one of his seven 'I am' statements: 'I am the light of the world' (Jn 8:12).

The need for light is paramount in human living. Without light we are in the dark:
- physically. We can only stumble along not being sure where we are going;
- intellectually. We cannot 'see' truth, reality. Light is analogously connected with knowledge and revelation which we term illumination;
- emotionally. Darkness, depression, release feelings of being heavyhearted.. Happiness on the other hand evokes a sense of lightheartedness.
- spiritually. Lack of light impedes our sense of the Divine whose image is one of great light/ lightsomeness. 'God is light' (1 Jn 1:5).

The Sun

The sun is the par excellence source of light in the world. This is largely taken for granted in the bible. The following texts have been chosen for their special symbolic imagery:

'High above he pitches a tent for the sun, who comes out of his pavilion like a bridegroom, exulting like a hero to run his race' (Ps 19:5,6). This is an image of the sun illuminating the earth but it also evokes the Incarnation and especially Jesus' resurrection. The sun is clearly used by Paul as a symbol of Jesus' resurrection as well as our own: 'The sun has its brightness, the moon a different brightness, and the stars a different brightness and the stars differ from each other in brightness. It is the same with the resurrection of the dead' (1 Cor 15:41).

The sun is used in a double negative sense as a symbol of the heavenly Jerusalem: 'The city did not need the sun or the moon for light, since it was lit by the radiant glory of God and the Lamb was a lighted torch for it' (Rev 21:23). This text also offers the image of the Son illuminating the Father.

The Moon

The moon has a 'life'; it is born, grows, decreases and dies. The 'death' of the moon is not final for after three days it rises again. Like the moon we live, grow and die, and our death is also not final. The new moon is born out of the death of the old moon. This lunar law governs the universe where every form becomes, regresses, dies and then rises.

'Now a great sign appeared in heaven: a woman, adorned with the sun, standing on the moon and with twelve stars on her head for a crown. She was pregnant' (Rev 12:1). The woman in this book represents the people of Israel - a covenanted, faithful, fruitful people who are the beloved of God. The symbolism here portrays the woman standing, full of vitality and not subject to the waxing and waning of time. She is constant and responds with constancy. The Catholic church in her liturgy applies this text to Mary.

The moon is taken as a symbol of beauty. A landscape lit up by a full moon can be ravishing - for example Jerusalem when lit by the paschal moon. 'Who is this arising like the dawn, beautiful as the moon?' (S. of S. 6:9).

The Stars

The people of the ancient near east were very conscious of the stars. A particular star could signify a God, usually in the form of a deified king, as we read in Balaam's oracle. His messianic

oracle speaks of the 'man with the far seeing eyes' (Nb 24:15,17). 'He sees what shaddai makes him see...I see him - but not in the present, a star from Jacob takes the leadership, a sceptre arises from Israel'. The 'star from Jacob' is a reference to the Davidic dynasty from which the Messiah would come.

Balaam's oracle was realised at Jesus' birth. 'We have seen his star in the east...the star went forward and halted over the place where the child was' (Mt 2:2).

Stars are symbols of a light which point a way forward. A long held belief is that the stars tell us something and this belief is also true of today. There is however a danger of a star cult which turns people away from God. In other words people act according to what their stars says as interpreted by astrologists or horoscope people.

RAINBOW, LIGHTNING

These are also symbols of light although they are not specifically mentioned in the creation story. A rainbow is light broken into its primary colours; lightning is light shattered into streaks. The first is an image of radiance and fidelity, the second of power and unpredictability.

Rainbow

The rainbow is revealed to Noah as a symbol of God's covenant with the whole planet earth. (See Gn 9:8-16). As a symbol of universalism it echoes today's idea of our global village; the earth is seen as our cosmic home. The rainbow is also a symbol of the faithfulness of God; of his commitment to preserve his creation.

In the Book of Revelation, John uses the symbol of the rainbow to highlight his overall imagery of the 'One who was sitting on the throne.. There was a rainbow encircling the throne and this looked like an emerald...' (4:3). It is this writer's way of giving an impression of a great and very beautiful light. It is also an image which shows that the end time - the destiny of all created being - is to be full of light. This is in sharp contrast to the universe's beginnings where all was darkness and chaos.

Lightning

Lightning is an image which can be used positively or negatively. Job asks: 'From which direction does the lightning fork when it scatter sparks over the earth?' (38:24).

With a lightning flash we see, then we don't see. As such it is an image of when we understand and then don't understand both our own reality and reality around us. It points to the disconcerting quality of human living. A sense of disconcertedness persists throughout life but as we age but it can be counteracted by growth in wisdom. Part of wisdom is the attainment of a rich simplicity; integration in the midst of and not apart from the complexities of life. It is coming to a certain synthesis in our lives, which is something different from compromise. Disconcertedness diminishes as wisdom grows. Wisdom can hold the contradictions of life in an inner contentment which is able to harmonize opposites.

The negative image that lightning can portray is that of evil presenting itself as a symbol of light - the area of deception and sin. In these frames the effect of sin is portrayed in the dead tree as it is shown in the sculpture struck by lightning and denuded of its leaves. It is hard, stark, lifeless. It stands out as different while at the same time remaining somewhat hidden as it insinuates itself among the other beautiful and truthful images that bring light and life. In other words sin can present itself under the form of 'an angel of light'. The prelude to sin, temptation, is aptly symbolised in the sculpture's cobweb. Cobwebs have a tendency to ensnare, draw in, capture, entangle and ultimately even strangle things in their web.

THE ELEMENTS - AIR, FIRE, WATER, EARTH

Air

Air is obviously not represented in this sculpture other than hinted at by the space created through the open design of the panels. Similarly we ourselves have to be made aware of the presence of air and this happens through *breath* and *wind*.

Wind can be strong or gentle. Storm force winds manifest God's power and majesty. 'From

the heart of the tempest Yahweh gave Job his answer' (Job 38:1). It is frightening at times to feel the wind's force, to have a sense of your body being blown by its power. A constructive use of wind power are windmills that convert the wind into another form of energy. Mild winds also reveal God, as in the gentle breeze which mediated Elijah's encounter with God. (See 1 Kg 19:11).

Fire

There are a great many references to fire in both Old and New Testaments. In the Old Testament there are three events which stress the important role fire plays in manifesting God's presence:

Abraham's covenant is ratified through the symbol of fire. (See Gn 15:7). Formalising contracts in ancient times was ritualised by the contracting parties passing between the parts of a slain animal. In this contract between God and Abraham, God makes his presence visible through the symbol of a firebrand: 'There appeared a smoking furnace and a firebrand that went between the halves'. Abraham would have understood what this sign meant: the firebrand was God sealing his side of the covenant. (See also Jer 34:18).

The *Pillar of Fire* was a crucial sign of God's presence with his people right from the moment they crossed the Red Sea. 'Yahweh went before them in the form of a pillar of cloud to show them the way and by night in the form of a pillar of fire to give them light' (Ex 13:12).

The *Burning Bush* was a key revelation of who God is and it particularly manifested the divine holiness. 'Yahweh appeared to him in the shape of a flame of fire coming from the middle of a bush. There was the bush blazing but it was not burnt up. Come no nearer, take off your shoes, the place on which you stand is holy ground' (Ex 3:2). This symbol of the presence of God made it a sacred place.

Fire is something which attracts, yet it is also feared. The phrase, 'don't play with fire' speaks for itself. Moses attempts to go close to the fire but God tells him to come no nearer.

Instinctively Moses responds by covering his face (Ex.3:6) since no one can gaze on God's majesty and live. This image brings home to us that in this life our encounter with God is never immediate. Our encounter is always mediated by something else such as a word, symbol, person, event, thought, or feeling. It can be mediated in a powerful way through silence.

The Law was given to Moses on *Sinai*. It was a solemn moment. 'To the eyes of the sons of Israel the glory of the Lord seemed like a devouring fire on the mountain top... The mountain of Sinai was entirely wrapped in smoke, because Yahweh had descended on it in the form of fire' (Ex 24;17, 19:18).

The sign of fire was also important in the New Testament:
Pentecost is the scene of the ratification of the New Covenant. 'Something appeared to them that seemed like tongues of fire; these separated and came to rest on the head of each of them'. In the light of the Old Testament events this symbol of fire was a powerful sign of God's presence inaugurating this new covenant.

Jesus made several references to fire:
'He [John the Baptist] will baptise you with the Holy Spirit and fire' (Lk 3:16).
'I have come to bring fire to the earth and how I wish it were blazing already' (Lk 12:19).
Surely Jesus here was speaking of the fire of the Spirit that inflames human hearts?
'Did not our hearts burn within us?' (Lk 24:32).
Jesus also spoke of the destructive power of fire: the fire of judgement.
Origen, a theologian of the early church, attributes the following saying to Jesus: 'He who is close to me is close to fire'.

W a t e r

In early biblical tradition God was envisaged as creating out of 'the deep' which was associated with water. Ancient creation stories are all linked with water in some way. The two great rivers the Tigris and Euphrates in Mesopotania (now Iraq) and the Nile in Egypt were always flooding. Chaos is always a possible threat in human existence and flooding became a symbol

of this. The creator God transformed this chaotic situation and created order in the world. Before this order was created we are given a picture of 'God's spirit hovered over the deep [water]' (Gn1:1). Since then water has been used as a symbol of a passage, a passage of transformation. We see such examples in the crossing of the Red Sea and in Baptism.

The ancient Israelites saw two sources of water and God controlled both floodgates. The first source came from on high and included rain, hail, snow and dew; (still an important water source for their vineyards). The second source came from below and included springs, rivers and seas. Rain and sea are depicted in this sculpture.

Water is essential to life; we are made up of 70% water. Having sufficient water in a country like Israel, especially in its desert areas, was a sign of God's blessing. Dryness, 'like a dry weary land without water' (Ps 63:1) is not a sign of blessing. A constant aspiration for water is aptly applied to our inner life in the Pentecost sequence phrase: 'On our dryness pour your dew'.

Jesus uses water as a symbol of the gift of God offered to each one. 'The water I shall give will turn into a spring inside him welling up to eternal life' (Jn 4:13,14). Jesus' revelation recorded at the end of the book of Revelation says 'All who want it may have the water of life and have it free' (22:17).

Torrents of water can be menacing and destructive. Waves can overwhelm us physically as well as inner waves destroying our spirit.

Earth

The earth has been considered under planet earth. There is also earth in the sense of the soil. The Hebrew word for soil or earth is 'adamah'. It is the symbol used for an essential ingredient in the creation of the human person. At the end of life the wisdom writer Qoheleth refers to man 'going to his everlasting home' and part of that process is 'the dust returns to the earth as it once came from it' (Eccles 12:5,6). The perishable side of human nature was acknowledge by other Old Testament writers. For instance Joshua says to his people as his death was approaching: 'And now today I must go the way of all the earth' (23:14).

Paul, while recognizing the perishable dimension of human existence sees that the resurrection has changed this fact. 'The first man, being from the earth, is earthly by nature; the second man is from heaven'. Through the power of resurrection everything is changed. - now 'the dead will be raised imperishable... our present perishable nature must put on imperishability and this mortal nature must put on immortality' (1 Cor 15:46,53).

Conclusion

It is appropriate to conclude this reflection on the universe with some words on *beauty* and *celebration*.

'Concern for *beauty* is not a moral cop-out. It leads us firmly into the midst of all that is going on in our world. Where there is beauty apparent, we are to enjoy it; where there is beauty hidden, we are to unveil it; where there is beauty defaced, we are to restore it; where there is not beauty, we are to create it'.[34]

'We cannot live without joy, and that is why I consider life, the universe, and the planet earth, all as a single, multiform, celebratory event. This capacity for *celebration* is of ultimate importance... That is one of the things religion can give: the gift of delight in existence. Such delight is a source of immense energy'.[35]

This conclusion also notes that we miss a great deal because we do not understand adequately biblical symbolism. Neither are we great at creating and using modern forms of symbols such as new liturgies, religious art, etc. Feminist groups have been creative in this area. The Eucharist has tended of late to become overly dominant as a form of worship in the Catholic church. As a result there has been a stunting of the development of other forms of

---

[34] R. McAffee Brown, quoted in 'Living spirit' in *The Tablet* 9 May 1998.
[35] T. Berry, quoted in 'Living spirit' in *The Tablet* 9 May 1998.

symbolic activities. There is need for non-sacramental or para liturgies to celebrate the many significant moments in people's lives and these need to be done in ways that are creative, fresh and meaningful.

Reflection

Do you find glimpses of God's creative activity in your ordinary everyday environment? What do these glimpses tell you about God?

Are you growing in appreciation of all that is created?

Are you coming to a deeper awareness of your co-creator role in the on-going work of creation?

What efforts are you making to improve the environment by, for example, using recycling opportunities like bottle banks, supporting moves for a cleaner environment, cultivating and beautifying your own area?

Creation Of Man And Woman

Sculpture

This 4,500 year old piece of yew sculpted by Michael Casey is a profound symbol of the creation of man and women. This tree lay in the earth, the boglands of Allen, until it was discovered by Michael who, with Yahweh the Master Craftsman, co-created it into its present form. Biblical echoes of 'I was by his side, a master craftsman, delighting him day after day, ever at play in his presence,... delighting to be with the sons of men' (Prov. 8:6) are clearly seen in Michael's description of his work.

Michael writes about how he worked on this particular piece. 'It was on a Christmas Eve we met, a low winter sun on your form excited me. I sat in awe beside you, you who had existed before Abraham was a boy. I sat and the winter sun left us and at last, out of your tangled mess, you spoke to me... you were no longer a growing tree but a fallen one, submerged in the boglands that had grown over you and I heard of your release into a strange new world, and you told me of a new reality you wished to become and I took you into my workshop and we worked together to create order out of chaos.

Often I would take you out on my trolley into my garden and allow the sun to light you up once more and in that fusion of sunlight and instinct you were no longer a piece of wood but a celebration of life, and when our task was done, we said goodbye and you left for your new home among the Wicklow mountains. I have often been asked to describe you in form and spirit... impossible... we who worked with a secret language must ask the beholder who gazes on you to listen very quietly and perhaps he too will be embraced by your spirit'.

The creation of 'order out of chaos' and the emergence of this work from the bowels of the earth show clear links with the creation story in general and the creation of man and woman in particular. The roots reveal the human person's rootedness to this earth. The upright form shows we are upright creatures, as well as the pinnacle of God's creation.

There is too a definite sexual symbolism - the open vagina and the erect penis -symbols of intimate lovemaking where man and woman become one in a special way. Portrayed also is a sense of nakedness - that original nakedness where there was no sense of shame or embarrassment. 'Both of them were naked, the man and his wife, but they felt no shame in front of each other.' (Gn 2:25). This is a particularly sensuous sculpture. People like to touch the wood, run their hand along it in a stroking fashion. One can indeed call it a symbol of sexuality.

This reflection focuses on three things - the biblical background to the story of the creation of man and woman, the unity of each person, and finally human sexuality.

Biblical Background

The first story of creation, known as the priestly version, notes that the climax of creation was reached in the human person. The text mentions divine consultation. The phrase 'let us' gives a hint of relationship within the Godhead: 'Let us make man in our own image, in the likeness of ourselves, and let them be masters of the fish of the sea, the birds of heaven, the cattle...' (Gn 1:26). Elohim is the word used in this text which is the plural name for God.

Note too plural use of the word 'man' when related to the word 'masters' in the above text. The creation of Adam includes both man and woman. This is expressed clearly in the following passage: 'God created man... in the image of God he created him, male and female he created them'. It notes specifically that the distinction of the sexes is of divine origin and so we are truly not just persons but sexual persons before God. The full meaning of the word 'Adam' is therefore only realized when it includes man and woman (vs. 26-27).

The first creation story in *Genesis* 1 speaks strongly of generativity and fecundity. In the second story, the *Genesis* 2 account, mutuality and intimacy are stressed. This second account known as the Yahwistic version was compiled first and it uses a figurative story format. The account is vivid and concrete and the perspective is earthy and human rather than cosmic and divine as in the Genesis 1. The setting is barren with the earth devoid of water for 'God had not yet sent rain on the earth' (2:5). Adam, namely man and woman are formed from *Adamah,* the

Hebrew word for soil, earth. The phrase 'taken from the earth' stresses we are part of creation and like all created beings we are perishable. The way the bible constantly expresses this is by saying we are 'flesh'. 'Flesh', like everything God creates, is something good, wholesome.

Flesh is therefore not an evil principle in us. Evil arises from our evil choices. The 'heart' is the biblical symbol used to express the inmost core of our being and it is from this heart place that evil inclinations and desires spring. They do not come from the body which is something inherently good.

This 'earthcreature' needed the breath of the living God, God's own living-giving force, to become a living being. 'Dusty earth was warmed to become a living being , male and female, by the divine breath'.[36] We cannot exist, or continue in existence as the image of God without this spiration or breath of God sustaining us in life. Neither can we continue after death without this spiration. This dependency on God is part of our essential make-up. We express this dependency by reliance on God and by obeying his laws - the laws that are inherent within human nature itself. The most basic laws are concerned with loving and respectful ways of relating to God, other people, ourselves and the earth.

Adam or man is a collective noun. For an Israelite 'Adam'/ Adam and Eve, are the ancestors of the human race and as such they carry within them the collectivity of the whole race. 'Adam', (man and woman), comes from the earth; 'Adam' will return to the earth. The earth is destined for 'Adam' to cultivate and use well. 'Adam' in this story is created with responsibility for three sets of relationships - with God, with human beings and with the earth. Everyone of us is responsible for these three sets of relationships.

God placed 'Adam' in a beautiful garden just as he places us in a beautiful world. Adam's mission and our mission is one of stewardship. God gave us a good creation. We can only

---

[36] Quotation from summer workshop notes. The workshop on Sexuality was given by Fran Herder and John Heagle in Marianella, Dublin, summer 1997. The seminar was based on their book: F. Herder and J. Heagle, *Your Sexual Self* (Indiana: Ave Maria Press 1992). Both authors are psychologists. Much of the material in this section is drawn from this workshop.

blame ourselves and not God for the woes that exist in the world. Except for natural disasters the majority of calamities are due to a misuse of human freedom.

The Unity of the Human Person

Hebrew thought was never dualistic. The separation of the person into body and soul, and the distinction between matter and spirit came with the Greek philosophers and their thinking infiltrated Christian thinking. Another form of dualism is the divide between this life and the after life.

What was and is clear in both the Old and New Testaments is that meaning to life is found in this life and not in the hereafter. A strong Jewish understanding is that life is lived now. This idea, central to the book of Ecclesiastes is also alive in today's committed Jewish believers. Jesus expresses the same notion and says it with great clarity: 'I have come that you may have life and have it to the full' (Jn 10). He was referring to this life as well as eternal life.

We are spiritual beings possessing intellect and will but we are earthbound by space through our bodily reality. We are historical beings and so are limited by time. We are strongly influenced by the culture we live in. We never fully possess ourselves; we're always becoming. But it is always the unique whole person who is becoming.

Sexuality

Since we are created with the distinction of being either male or female our sexuality is of fundamental importance. *Sexuality lies at the heart of who we are.*

Sexuality has for everyone two inherent factors:
Firstly, there is the call/demand *to give life*; to be creative or more accurately co-creative. An essential part of being human is to be a life-giver and to remain a life giver to the end of our lives.

Secondly, there is the call *to be intimate*. Intimacy is essentially about being close to another or other human beings. True intimacy is mutual and is concerned with engagement - the

engagement of giving and receiving love. Genital intimacy is a particular way of being intimate but it is only one form of expression. It offers the possibility of being sexuality's most profound expression but this possibility may not always be experientially true in practice.

Sexuality is therefore about relationships. It involves interpersonal communication in both same sex as well as other sex relationships. There is the assumption that sexuality is only for within partnerships that engage in genital activity. If people are not within such relationships there is at times an insinuation that such persons are asexual. Children, single people, vowed celibates, homosexuals, people with genital disability, older people, widows and widowers - all of us are sexual beings and remain so to the very end of this life.

We are sexual in everything we do, say and are; we cannot not be sexual beings. Of necessity we reach out to others; seek communion at one level or another. Our sexuality is what gives us *energy for relationships*. It is the power inherent in our makeup as man or woman which urges, impels us, to seek connection with each other. It is an energy for encounter, for creativity. Sexuality is not primarily about seeking personal satisfaction, rather it's concern is directed towards others. This energy released by our sexuality is an 'other-orientating' energy.

Ethics today reflects on the importance of human relationships in the whole area of sexuality. There is now a turning away from the emphasis on an act-orientated ethics to a personalist-relational one. There is also a deepening of understanding of the difference between genitality and sexuality. *Sexuality* is broader and more inclusive. It is about what we do, or don't do with our hearts. We express our sexuality in how we listen, disclose, be with other people. *Genitality* is about particular sexual behaviours that people engage in.

For those who live in a committed partnership which involves genital expression the making public of that relationship through the contract of marriage has always been considered as something desirable. It benefits the couple as well as contributes to enhancing stability in community and state life. For Christians revelation clearly points to the sacrament of marriage as being the proper ambiance for the living out of this chosen way of life. This sacrament offers special graces to enrich the love between wife and husband throughout their entire married life. Genitality can precede and even take the place of sexuality when there is no relational content present. People in this situation are physically naked with each other but with no sense of responsibility. To be a truly sexual person is more demanding - it is about *undressing our hearts* - being emotionally naked with people, and especially the significant other or others in our lives.

In practice this means taking responsibility to share, to '*undress our heart*' from a level we are comfortable with while at the same time moving in the direction of stretching ourselves further. We are always becoming more mature sexual persons and the constant question that this presents us with is: how are we doing with our loving? It is good to reflect in a personal way on our relational experiences in order to see what energy is there and what we are doing with our sexual energy. Do we use it to build others up, or is our use of it diminishing others in some way by certain destructive attitudes, words or deeds?

It is not good, as the bible says, for the 'earth creature', Adam, to be alone. Hence we should not move in the direction of isolation, of cutting ourselves off from others, since this is destructive of becoming human. Even hermits must retain close bonds with people as they live apart in their hermitage. Our sexuality carries us past isolation and autonomy to community. To be human is to be in relation, to be connected not disconnected with others, nor unconnected with the planet itself.

Cosmic energy is generated by the power of attraction, for example the pull of gravity, photosynthesis, osmosis. Sexuality is part of that cosmic power of allurement. Indeed cosmic allurement becomes conscious in humans. It is a power which mysteriously draws us to another/others.

Spirituality and sexuality, as seen in the creation story, are friends not enemies. The whole movement of God is into creation, into flesh. God is better than us at that. Our effort is sometimes too 'spiritual' and not sufficiently earthed, enfleshed. Sexuality and mysticism are

closely linked, and people are often suspicious of both. For example they share a common language using words like yearning, longing, passion, compassion, seeking the beloved, as well as sharing common poetic images and symbols such as fire and flame. The strongest link between sexuality and spirituality is that both these dimensions of our humanity contain enormous sources of energy. Either source can use that energy for good or ill.

We are always in the process of becoming from the moment of conception until death. When the ovum and sperm meet cell division occurs. As the multiplication of cells proceeds so too does the process of differentiation of cell types. Embryology shows that at the early beginnings we are sexually undifferentiated, namely the genital buds are the same. As the foetus grows sexual differences appear. Accepting our sexual orientation and owning and experiencing our own unique attractiveness is an inherent part of accepting our personal existence and full human living includes becoming more mature sexual persons. It is desirable that we become more masculine or more feminine as we grow older and are able to express this in deeper forms of intimacy, be it, for instance, with one's spouse, partner, friend or grandchild.

Intimacy can be transliterated as 'in-to-me-see'. It is about being close enough to let another see inside of me and to let myself see inside another. This level of communion fills us with wonder, but at the same time scares us. We seek human connectedness while at the same time this can be found threatening. Intimacy is not for the fainthearted.

The universal game of peek-a-boo initiates the beginning of communion. In learning the art of self-revelation the first step is: you can see me; the second step follows: I will be in charge of my own self-disclosure. The child catches the eye contact of an adult, holds it, and then looks away, usually turning the whole head as it does so. As trust builds up the child can hold the contact made for longer periods. In all of us and throughout our lives as trust grows we allow others to see us more intimately, and this includes warts and all. We allow our vulnerability to be seen; are able to share on it with another; and are able to facilitate others as they share their vulnerability with us.

Such self-disclosure produces intimacy. It is about sharing my visions, dreams, feelings, needs, vulnerability. Intimacy is all about making love and there are thousands of ways of doing this other than genital sex. We make love with a look, gestures, words, caring activities etc.

Intimacy can only be built on equality, never on dependency. Sexual abuse damages this process of self-disclosure since trust, mutuality and the sense of being safe are obliterated. Abuse is when someone with more power meets their needs at the expense of the person with little or no power. Violence/ invasiveness is the fundamental sin against relationships since equality and mutuality are non-existent.

A temptation of adulthood in relation to our sexual self is to settle into patterns, into set ways of relating. 'There is a whole lot of music inside of us and the greatest sin is to die with that song unsung'. Those who express intimacy in its genital form can also settle into patterns that are no longer as expressive as they used to be. Meaningful changes require change on the part of two people. This is difficult to achieve without honest communication between both partners.

It is necessary to foster good communications from the very beginning of loving relationships. Hurts of the past and unfulfilled areas in our lives may never be noted, faced or spoken about. Developing freedom in intimate human relating and the ability to look outwards from the relationship are factors which enhance growth within the partnership as well as personal growth. A wisdom saying on love by de Mello is apt: 'A newly married couple said, "What shall we do to make our love endure?" Said the Master, "Love other things together"'.[37]

Characteristics of an integrated sexual life include: a healthy self-esteem, interpersonal warmth, compassion, tenderness, gentleness, flexibility, an ability to take risks, being able to play well. Such people are comfortable with themselves and others. Other people can often sense this comfort radiating from them as they make it easy to be in their company. Persons with an integrated sexuality are at home in their bodies and in their spirit.

---

[37] A. de Mello, *One Minute Wisdom* (Anand: Anand Press 1987) 111.

Unintegrated sexuality's characteristics include: having low or grandiose self-esteem, overly judgmental attitudes towards others, a subtle lack of genuineness, being over-critical, careless or overly cautious, secretive, super orthodox.

Compartmentalization in living is likely to occur when our sexual energy does not fit with our beliefs, feelings, commitments. Our sense of at-homeness with our sexual self or a lack of it, profoundly effects how comfortable we are not only with ourselves and others but with how comfortable we are with the choices we make and the life style we lead.

The gospel mandate is a call to go out and make love in the world. We make love when we act with God as 'co-creators, co-shapers, and co-stewards'[38] of the world. Such love has the power to transform even the bleakest situation. Love, on the positive side can transform ourselves and our ability to relate to others in ways we could never even imagine. Love can also transform the negative since love alone has the power of healing ills and undoing the evil of decline. We manifest this love with our whole sexual self, expressing it through words, gestures, presence, actions, silence as well as genitally if this is appropriate to the relationship.

R e f l e c t i o n

Reflect on the givens of your person, especially your sex, your gifts and the uniqueness of your personality.

Do you experience yourself as an attractive person? Can you say with the psalmist 'for the wonder of my being I thank you Lord'. (Ps.139:14)?

Reflect on your relational life. How loving are you? do you give life? are you growing in intimacy?

How creatively do you use the gifts of your own unique personality?

---

[38] Terms used by A. Carr, an American feminist theologian, in *Transforming Grace: Christian Tradition and Women's Experience* (New York: Harper and Row 1988).

Mother And Child

Sculpture

Noel Scullion's work, which he titles 'Dreamer's Rest', portrays a mother and child - in fact his wife and their firstborn son. Both are asleep with their faces touching each other conveying, he feels, 'peace, harmony, "oneness"'. The convex and concave outline of the mother and child on the ends of this divided seat, the level from which one views the piece, the wetness or dryness of the stone (which alters its colour) and above all the play of sunlight or its absence, highlight in differing ways the faces of these two figures.

Introduction

This reflection primarily focuses on the child. This and the following three sections have a common thread: we exist throughout our lives as unique individuals while at the same time we can only become fully human through relationships, through being loved. The three relationships considered are parent and child, significant other with significant other, and community relationships. In all these key relationships there can be a tendency to over-idealize them. The truth can be that much in the actual experiencing of human relating is messy and painful as well as being satisfying and joyfilled.

This dual process of being-unique and being-in-relationship starts in the womb where the baby develops its unique characteristics while at the same time experiencing a bonding with the mother. It shares the rhythm of the mother's heart beat and in the later stages of pregnancy grows in alertness to hearing sound, sensing pain, and possibly to picking up the mother's mood concerning her baby within.

It is fortunate if at the birth the father is there to receive the child and from then on that the nurturing and bonding is shared by both parents.

The outline of this reflection starts with the child in scripture, followed by some thoughts on the characteristics of children. A theology of childhood is then presented and finally there is a section on being a child of God.

The Child in Scripture

In the Old Testament the birth of a child is a sign of God's special blessing. In the bible the 'little ones' are those specially favoured by God.

Hosea specifically expresses God's tender love for children when he uses a child as an image of Israel. 'When Israel was a child I loved him' (Hos 11:1-5).

God chose certain children as special messengers of his revelation. Little Samuel receives the word of God. (1 S 3:1-21). The young David is chosen in preference to his older brothers to be king of Israel. (See 1 S 16:1-13). The young boy Daniel was filled with the Spirit and showed more wisdom than the elders in saving Susanna. (See Dn 13:44-50).

One of the psalms gives the lovely image of dependence, surrender to God, in the picture of a child in its mother's arms - something similar to the sculpture, the child resting against his mother - asleep. 'Enough for me to keep my soul tranquil and quiet like a child in its mother's arms, as content as a child that has been weaned' (131:2).

In the New Testament we see the saviour *Jesus came as child*. He was born in a cave, presented in the temple, was obedient to his parents. *Simeon:* 'You see this child: he is destined for the fall and for the rising of many in Israel, destined to be a sign that is rejected' (Lk 2:34). *Anna* 'spoke of the child to all who looked forward to the deliverance of Jerusalem' (Lk 2:38). Jesus experienced all the limitations of being a child, and like us had to grow 'in wisdom, age and grace' (Lk 2:52).

As an adult Jesus affirms children:
- He sees children as disciples - 'to them the kingdom belongs' (Mk 10:15).
- Children are special signs of his presence: 'Anyone who welcomes a little child like this in my name welcomes me' (Mt 18:5).

He also showed the importance of retaining our childhood

- Jesus tells us that we must receive the gift of his kingdom as a child receives gifts, namely with simplicity and trust. Children know they own nothing of themselves.
- The secret of true greatness is making oneself little and humble like a child: 'I tell you solemnly, unless you change and become like children you will never enter the kingdom of heaven. And so the one who makes himself as little as this little child is the greatest in the kingdom of heaven' (Mt 18:3,4).
- God's important secrets are revealed to those who have the heart of a child: 'I bless you, Father, Lord of heaven and earth, for hiding these things from the learned and the clever and revealing them to mere children. Yes, Father, for that is what it pleased you to do. Everything has been entrusted to me by my Father; and no one knows the Son except the Father, just as no one knows the Father except the Son and those to whom the Son chooses to reveal him' (Mt 11:25-27).

Jesus is stern about how adults relate with children

'Anyone who is an obstacle to bring down one of these little ones who have faith in me would be better drowned in the depths of the sea with a great millstone round his neck' (Mt 18:6).

Characteristics of Children

We learn characteristics of children from scripture and particularly from our own experience. They include: trust, simplicity, playfulness, openness, spontaneity, reliance on others, exploring, questioning - the ever constant 'why' question of the toddler! Not to be forgotten is a child's sensitivity so that as well as their keen ability to experience joy and delight they can also experience profound levels of pain and their very vulnerability opens them to this possibility.

Jean Vanier is recognized as a man who has a great affinity and concern for the 'little ones' in society. He writes movingly about children and expresses his tenderness and concern for them in poetic form in the following extracts:[39]

- 'a tiny child needs not only food and shelter but something more..much more.. a feeling of love that someone cares for him, ready to die for him, that he is really loved, that he is important...precious and so he begins to live, begins to sense the value of his being, and so it is that life rises in him and he grows in confidence in himself and in his possibilities of life and of creation'.

- 'Approach the child, not haughtily but humbly, not judging but loving, determined not to dominate, not even to give things rather to give myself, my time, energy and heart, and to listen believing that he is important, a child of God in whom Jesus lives. Approach with tenderness, gently, gently giving one's friendship, delicate soothing hands'.

- 'Life needs delicate gentle hands, hands that know just the right amount of water for life, just the right degree of light at the right time..or else, no life, no flower, no fruit..To evolve, life does need security in the mother, in the father, in the home'.

- 'Life needs security and hope; security being the fundamental basis, the earth in which life is born; hope being that call... to light and love and beauty... universality, shades of the infinite'.

'Towards a Theology of Childhood'[40]

To parents and those who work with or have contact with children Rahner says '... always and in all circumstances loving them'.

He speaks of the unique and unrepeatable value attached to childhood when most of our life

[39] J. Vanier, *Tears of Silence*, (New Jersey: Dimension Books 1970). Hereafter *Tears of Silence*. Jean Vanier is French and is the founder of over seventy L'Arche communities world-wide who offer community residences for people with learning disabilities.

[40] All the Rahner Quotations in this section are taken from 'Towards a Theology of Childhood' in *Theological Investigations* Vol. 8. Rahner says his aim in writing this article was to consider 'what the divinely revealed word has to say about childhood. In the intention of the Creator and Redeemer of children what meaning does childhood have, and what task does it lay upon us for the perfecting and saving of humanity? That is the question before us'. 33.

generated by the self-expression of the Father. We comprehend better the mystery of childhood if we see its foundation within this childhood of God. We are made into God's image like the Son. Through concretely living out our God-intended place of being 'sons/[daughters] in the Son', the more we become an expression of who God is, like Jesus did.

Jesus showed, by the way he lived out his own mature childhood, how we are to live ours. He did so by living moment by moment his filial relationship with his Abba, who is also our Father. He never anticipated the will of his Father but received it as events and his personal insights unfolded. He did so always in a spirit of gratitude, 'I thank you Father'... (Jn 11:41) for what is, for what is to come... Being like Jesus, in the way he lived out his filial relationship, is a core element in our following of Him.

This being received by grace into the family of God means also we are brothers and sisters to each member of the human race. Owning our childhood is both an adventure but also a responsibility that demands we operate out of that responsibility in an ever more mature way. This is essentially shown in our caring of others and particularly the needy members of the human family.

The dignity of the small child is thus without measure since that is where the mystery of a person's life begins. The church radicalises this dignity in a special way in infant baptism. Here the child is formally received into the family of God. A significant part of the ceremony are the words 'Ephrata' - 'be opened'. It is a symbol not only of the opening of the ears to hear but also of being open to receive the fullness of life that is on offer to each one. Jesus said: 'I have come that you may have life and have it to the full' (Jn 10:8).

One who is a good receiver, like a child, is a grateful person. When gratitude predominates as an individual faces death we see a profound expression of mature childhood lived to the end. Movingly, D. Nicholl wrote in his journal as he prepared for his own death: 'When you are full of gratitude there isn't room for anything else; there isn't room for recrimination and desire for revenge and things like that... My gratitude.. has in a way transformed my life, in the way I look back on my life. I am full of gratitude.'[44]

Reflection

Reflect on your childhood; on its joys and pain. Try to consciously own your past history, both its good and difficult happenings and then gently try to move further along the acceptance journey of that history which has made you into who you are now. Note in particular the strengths you have developed, not despite but rather because of, that history. Finally try to live ever more fully your present history and be open to the many possibilities for growth that are always available.

Reflect on your present experience of the child within you and the degree of maturity to which this child has come. Namely ponder on your present levels of openness, trustful submission, readiness to journey into unchartered waters etc.

Are you open to owning the truth that your most precious possession is to be a child of God? Do you admit to the implications of this: that your reliance on God is deepening; that you are becoming more aware that all your relationships are founded and built on respect knowing that each person is your brother or sister since all of us are children of God.

---

[44] D. Nicholl, *The Testing of Hearts, A Pilgrims Journey* (London; Darton, Longman and Todd 1998) 237. Hereafter *Testing of Hearts*, Donald Nicholl was president of the Ecumenical Institute at Tantur Jerusalem. These words in the final section titled 'Testing unto Death' were written just before he died.

Lovers

Sculpture

The sculpture centres on the intimate love that flows between two people, a man and woman in this instance. Imogen Stuart depicts this love by two hands: one male and the other female. 'These belong to two persons - rather like a pair of lovers in an embrace. This piece of sculpture is not only a sign and symbol of affection. To me it is affection or love per se....The human face as a carrier of an expression has lost to me a certain degree of its meaning... Hands are for me a much better vehicle for expressing emotions and ideas'.

These hands were carved out of a hard piece of yew that was 'knotted, wild and treacherously grown'. It took Imogen several years to complete this difficult work of chiselling away while finishing other pieces in between - a great symbol of endurance, a quality of love. 'Lovers' can be seen as symbolizing the union of man and woman in love. It reveals their interlocking, yet separateness; strength yet tenderness; equality yet difference. Above all it expresses the mutuality that is present in all true forms of adult love. Such mutuality is present in deep friendship and so this sculpture is also a symbol of friendship relationships whether they are between the same or opposite sex friends.

This reflection centres on two things - the theology of love and the relation of love. The latter leans on the thinking of Martin Buber and ends with an extract from the story The Velveteen Rabbit.

Theology of Love

Paul in his letter to the Corinthians has a great hymn to the beauty and wonder of love. Spicq says this is the most important passage on love in the New Testament. His translation is the following:

'Love is patient; love is kind; love is not envious; love does not brag; love is not conceited; love is not ill-mannered; love is not self-seeking; love is not irritable; love takes no note of injury;

love is not glad when injustice triumphs; it is glad when truth prevails; love is always ready to make allowances; always ready to trust, always to hope, always to be patient; love will never end'... 'You must want love more than anything else' (1 Cor. 13: 4-8).[45]

Love is a deeply theological term since 'God is love' (1Jn 4:16). A key expression of this divine love is God giving us the person infinitely dear to him: his Son Jesus. 'God [the Father]loved the world so much that he gave his only Son' (Jn 3:16). The Son showed the depth of his love by his emptying himself in becoming human in the first instance; by his selfless form of human living and by giving up his life for the salvation of all humankind. A most profound expression of Jesus' love, is when like his Father, he shares with us his own deepest love: the love of his Father. 'May the love with which you loved me be in them' (Jn 17:26).

Human existence comes to its highest fulfilment through loving relationships and Christianity's core message shows that God's love for each human person became concrete in the person of Jesus. Ultimately all love comes from God and flows back to God. If we reflect on our own loving and specific acts of love we know that our love is a power within us that is greater than ourselves. In other words when we act lovingly we exercise the transcendent within ourselves.

Human love while finite is personal; it is the core expression of who we are. It is this personal aspect that makes our love replicate divine love. Love, whether human or divine, is something warm, tender, compassionate and passionate and leads to the deepest form of human satisfaction that can be experienced in life. Throughout our lives we long for love, for closeness, for 'whole-heartedness'. B. Kennelly[46] speaks of the abundance of 'half-heartedness' that exists and the dearth of 'whole-heartedness'. The search for love, the wanting to be significant to the important other(s) in our lives continues over the modern person's ever lengthening life spans.

---

[45] C. Spicq, *Agape in the New Testament* (St. Louis: Herder and Herder 1965) Vol. 2. 139. Ceslaus Spicq is a French biblical scholar.
[46] Brendan Kennelly is an Irish poet. He spoke these words on a T.V. programme.

Becoming more human demands that we grow in love of God and others to the end of our lives. In the second half of life we will need to cope with our failures in the area of love and remain open to love's on-going challenges. As Vanier says 'Love is the greatest of all risks - the giving of myself, but do I dare take this risk?'[47]

Our relationships are inevitably experienced and expressed differently as the years pass. 'We cannot live the afternoon of life according to the programme of life's morning'. Loving relationships constantly require a redirection of energy if there is to be growth. Over time the outward expression of our love changes. Hopefully for instance the driveness of life diminishes as we grow older and move on to a more celebratory form of living where we become more 'human beings' rather than 'human doings'. Every relationship contains two contrasting qualities - fragility and resilience. Again as love matures we tend to become more aware of these dual aspects in our loving.

Relation of Love

We have reflected on sexuality and seen it as energy for relationships. That reflection on man and women centred on the physical and especially the emotional aspects of love - the undressing of the heart. This reflection on 'Lovers' focuses on the spiritual dimensions of love. It examines what we mean by relation; the bond that exists between two people who love each other. The relation, that dynamic reality, that space between two people, allows two unique individuals to meet is a bond which we call love. Relation is that intangible 'something', a reality of intensity, a spirit-filled bond which unites two people in a special way.

The encounter, the bond, the relation between the Father and the Son is one of intimate love and this love is what we call the Holy Spirit. Human relationships are akin to the Trinitarian relations since the bond that exists between two people who love each other is also spiritual. It is truly Spirit-filled.

Vanier expresses the love relation as follows: 'An encounter is a strange and wonderful thing,

---

[47] *Tears of Silence* 74.

presence one person to another, present one to another, life flowing one to another'.[48]

D. Nicholl speaks about loving relationships in terms of presence. 'Presence, total presence of one to another, is what is ultimate, so there comes a time when, having come into the presence, you have to stop thinking, otherwise you lose the awareness of the other'. He had just said a paragraph before: 'I don't mean that one doesn't have to think but it is a sign of imperfection; for if you know, you don't have to think. If you are in the presence of the loved one, you don't have to construct thoughts about the loved one: you just have to gaze'.[49]

To understand the profound nature of relationships we turn to Martin Buber. Buber was a Jew, a philosopher, and also a poet and a mystic who lived well into the turn of this century. His masterpiece and now classic work is *I and Thou*.[50] This book is solely concerned with relationship - both human and divine.

He speaks of three realities to which we relate:
- nature: where the communication is below the level of speech.
- people: where the communication is normally through speech or gesture.
- God: where the communication is clouded and when most profound is often through the medium of silence. 'We perceive no Thou but nonetheless we feel we are addressed and we answer... We speak the primary word with our being, though we cannot utter Thou with our lips'.

Our whole existence is concerned with relating but the prime concern of this reflection is our relation with persons. We relate in two different ways: one is with an impersonal manner when we perceive the other as an 'It', or when we relate personally the other becomes 'Thou'. The former, the I-It relationship, considers the other thing/person as something to be 'used' and therefore as a *means* to something else, whereas the second, the I-Thou relationship is

---

[48] Ibid. 76.
[49] *Testing of Hearts* 234.
[50] All Buber quotations in this section are taken from *I and Thou*.

about persons and the concern is with *an end* - 'meeting'. These two categories of relating run through all human activity.

Buber considers both I-Thou and I-It as one word. The hyphen between the words makes them form a single word so that one part of the word cannot exist without the other. Each word signifies one of two ways of relating. The 'I' part of the word differs depending on whether it is hyphenated with 'Thou' or 'It'. The I-Thou word establishes the world of relation. It is the primary word and it can only be spoken by our whole being. The I-It word can never be spoken by our whole being. When I use the word I, I take my stance within it in relation to an It or a Thou. The It always has boundaries but the Thou has no bounds. Experience belongs to the I-It word and human experience always contains limits. The I-Thou word which constitutes relationship has no bounds since it is a spiritual reality.

When I address another human person as a Thou that person is no longer a thing among things or a person among persons, rather, 'all else lives in his/[her] light'. 'I do not experience the man to whom I say Thou. But I take my stand in relation to him, in the sanctity of the primary word... Here is the cradle of Real Life'. Since the primary word is spoken with our whole being it means we withhold nothing of ourselves. The relation with which I stand towards Thou is real; it affects me and I affect it.

My stepping out towards Thou and the Thou that comes to meet me is through grace. It is not found by seeking. It never takes place solely through my reaching out, but neither can it take place without me. Buber adds in his postscript to the 1957 edition of *I-Thou* that the I-Thou relation 'is a grace, for which one must always be ready and which one never gains as an assured possession'.

I become through my relation to the Thou; as I become I, I say Thou. All real living is meeting.[51] And such a meeting is immediate, or as Buber says 'direct'; nothing intervenes between the I and the Thou and everything that is indirect becomes irrelevant. I am most myself, most complete,

---

[51] All italics and underlinings in the Buber quotations in this section are mine.

when I can utter Thou to another person.

Love is the bond that exists between I and Thou. Feelings of love which often vary in kind and intensity may accompany this reality but they do not constitute the relation. 'Love is responsibility of an I for a Thou'. This relation is one of mutuality - both 'Thous' affect the other. Saying Thou to another means seeing the whole being of the other. It is always a word of affirmation.

Inevitably every Thou becomes an It at times simply because we cannot sustain the intensity of the Thou experience. The Thou which can only be Thou - namely God, (since it is impossible for God to relate in an It manner) can sadly from the human side of human/divine relating become an It. There is a human tendency in both our relating and speaking about God to make God an It.

The I-Thou word arises out of a natural combination of the antenatal child with its mother. The I-It word arise out of the natural separation that occurs at birth. Over time relation replaces the severance of that primary natural connection. The natural instinct is to make every relationship into a Thou since our beginning starts in relation.

Early relating in the womb is achieved first by touch, then sound and after birth visually. Hugging a teddy bear (physical touch) and the peak-a-boo game (visual/emotional 'touch') are examples of a continuation of this process. 'The development of the soul in the child is inextricably bound up with that of the longing for the *Thou* with the satisfaction and disappointments of this longing'. But it is only by entering into relationships that the child develops. '*Through the Thou a man becomes I.*' Cardinal Hume puts it this way; '"I" needs "we" to be really "I"' and adds 'we are persons in relationship; we are better persons as those loving relationships grow'.[52]

There is a sense in relating with realities other than persons, that those relations can have a

[52] Basil Hume, 'Our restless society: finding a cure' in *The Tablet*, 13th June 1998.

certain I-Thou quality about them. When we 'meet', as opposed to 'use' what exists in the world, be it a particular animal, a tree etc, we discover our solidarity with nature. Each meeting with reality prepares us for further meetings.

The world of It is the world in which we live out our lives in time and space. However in this ordinary everyday world moments of the Thou break in on us and 'appear as strange lyric and dramatic episodes, seductive and magical, but tearing us away to dangerous extremes, loosening the well-tried context, leaving more questions than satisfaction behind them'. Buber then continues with this strong stark statement:

In all the seriousness of truth, hear this: without It man cannot live. But he who lives with
It alone is not a man.

'Spirit in its human manifestation is a response of man to his Thou....*Spirit is not in the I but between I and Thou*'. Hence living a Spirit-filled life means living a relational life. We live in the Spirit if we enter into relation with our Thou with our whole being. The Spirit is not manifest, it simply is. 'God's speech to men penetrates what happens in the life of each one of us, and all that happens in the world around us.. Happening upon happening, are enabled and empowered by the personal speech of God to demand of the human person that he take his stand and make his decision'. In other words we do not meet God alongside or above the happenings of our everyday lives, but rather we meet God within those very happenings.

In particular 'through contact with every Thou we are stirred with a breath of the Thou that is of eternal life. This is the deepest energy that arises from within the relationship between lovers'.

Marriages, partnerships, friendships and loving relationships of all kinds occur and are given new life by 'the revealing by two people of the Thou to one another. Out of this a marriage is built up by the Thou that is neither of the I's'. All of us, simply because we are human, swing between Thou and It. It is important that we cross again and again the threshold of the Thou place where our spirit is kindled anew. We then return to the It place renewed by this spark.

Conclusion

The wonder of relation, relating, relationships, is delightfully expressed in the story of a child's relation with his toy rabbit. The story illustrates that relationships are what is most real in life. It is the relation in turn that makes us Real.

'Nursery magic is very strange and wonderful, and only those playthings that are old and wise and experienced like the Skin Horse understand all about it.

"What is REAL?" asked the Rabbit one day, when they were lying side by side near the nursery fender, before Nana came to tidy the room. "Does it mean having things that buzz inside you and a stick-out handle?"

"Real isn't how you are made," said the Skin Horse. "It's a thing that happens to you. When a child loves you for a long, long time, not just to play with, but REALLY loves you, then you become Real." "Does it hurt?" asked the Rabbit. "Sometimes," said the Skin Horse for he was always truthful. "When you are Real you don't mind being hurt." "Does it happen all at once, like being wound up," he asked, "or bit by bit?"

"It doesn't happen all at once," said the Skin Horse. "*You become*. It takes a long time. That's why it doesn't often happen to people who break easily, or have sharp edges, or who have to be carefully kept. Generally by the time you are Real, most of your hair has been loved off, and your eyes drop out and you get loose in the joints and very shabby. But these things don't matter at all, because once you are Real you can't be ugly, except to people who don't understand."

"I suppose you are Real?" said the Rabbit. And then he wished he had not said it, for he thought the Skin Horse might be sensitive. But the Skin Horse only smiled.

"The Boy's uncle made me Real" he said. "That was a great many years ago' but once you are Real you can't become unreal again. It lasts for always".

The Rabbit sighed. He thought it would be a long time before this magic called Real happened to him. He longed to become Real, to know what it felt like; and yet the idea of growing shabby and losing his eyes and whiskers was rather sad. He wished that he could become it without these uncomfortable things happening to him.'

Over time it did happen...

'The little Rabbit grew very old and shabby, but the Boy loved him just as much. He loved him so hard that he loved all his whiskers off, and the pink lining to his ears turned grey, and his brown spots faded. He even began to lose his shape, and he scarcely looked like a rabbit any more, except to the Boy. To him he was always beautiful, and that was all that the little Rabbit cared about. He didn't mind how he looked to other people, because the nursery magic had made him Real, and when you are Real shabbiness doesn't matter'.[53]

Reflection

Savour some of your special I-Thou moments with others and with God.

Where are you now in your life with your loving? Are there areas, times, when you are afraid to take the risk of loving, for fear of being misunderstood, rejected?

Do you appreciate and trust your God-given ability to love, to be real with another(s)? Do you allow another, others, God to 'meet' you as Thou?

[53] M. Williams, *The Velveteen Rabbit*, (London: Mammoth 1922) 8, 9, 21. Margery Williams is English and author of children's books.

Community

Sculpture

This sculpture by Alexander Sokolov is titled dancers. It suggests a spirit of joy that flows from togetherness. The experience of the interconnectedness of human life, manifested in the bonds created by belonging to community of whatever kind, is aptly expressed by the symbol of group dance. In this sculpture the form of each figure is different. Especially notable are the differing outlines of the space between each figure suggesting the uniqueness of each relationship while at the same time the group gives an overall sense of harmony and balance.

The interaction between each dancer coupled with the group acting as one provides a symbol of the great dance of life which as community we perform together. Dance is an art form that elicits a great sense of freedom. Jesus has told us he has come to set us free, to liberate all who are captive in any way. Dancing the great dance of life together is a great expression of that freedom which Jesus offers to all of us and especially when as communities we gather specifically in his name to celebrate our togetherness.

Introduction

Today the term 'community' is much used. One hears about the Local community, National community, European community, International Community; as well as the family community, the neighbourhood community, the church community. However what is meant by the concept community is often unclear. People's expectations about what it offers and more importantly the personal responsibility required to create it are fundamental issues that require constant discernment and creativity.

In general people realize we are social beings and that this necessitates a degree of interdependence and co-operation. The thinking, attitudes and behaviours that flow from our interconnectedness do not seem to exist to the degree that is desirable both for the good of the individual as well as the good of the human race down to our most basic community unit - the family. Our very understandings of such communities, in particular the family, are changing.[54] In today's sophisticated world, individualism and personal autonomy can take preference over the good of the community. The consequences of this is that both the individual and the community are diminished.

This reflection commences on what is meant by the term community. This is followed by a section on the church community under the headings scripture and community, Vatican II on community. Finally two aspects of the church community are considered, namely, that it is a pilgrim community and a community of sinners.

What Do We Mean by Community?

The differences between the terms Society and Community

Society and social order are based on the notion of differences which are harmoniously interrelated for the good of society. *Community* is based on what people have in common; it is formed, held together, and builds itself by shared meanings, particularly the shared meaning of a common vision. Divergent meaning divides community. Such divisions may be peripheral due to facts such as a diversity of culture or competencies. Serious divisions within a community can lead to people being radically opposed to each other and when this happens community can simply fail to exist.

Community is the ideal basis for society and without some form of community society will not survive. Disorder in society results from disruption in that society's expressions of community life, such as the family and the multiplicity of other groupings. These include church communities such as parish, religious societies and religious life communities.

Community is based on the sharing of common meaning

---

[54] What constitutes a family? - partners who have a child? single parent and child? married people without a child? heterosexual as well as homosexual partners in long term relationships?

Community is a human reality in the sense that it is constituted by the very things that make each individual human since they form the basis of human consciousness. These are experience, understanding, judgement and decision. A group of people form a community to the extent that common experience, common ways of understanding, common judgements and the ability to take decisions in common are present.

Lonergan puts this well: "Community is not just an aggregate of individuals within a frontier, for that overlooks its formal constituent, which is common meaning. Such common meaning calls for a common field of experience and, when that is lacking, people get out of touch. It calls for common or complementary ways of understanding and, when they are lacking, people begin to misunderstand, to distrust, to suspect, to fear, to resort to violence. It calls for common judgements and, when they are lacking, people reside in different worlds. It calls for common values, goals, policies and, when they are lacking, people operate at cross purposes."[55]

This means in practice that when some of these elements are absent, for example, if a person is away from a community for a lengthy period without any form of communication they will find themselves out of touch because they have not shared in the community's experiences. Likewise if there is not some form of common understanding, misunderstandings will arise which are disruptive of community. Certainly if there are not common judgements people live in different worlds on possibly a whole range of issues. Finally when there is an inability to take decisions in common people can find themselves diametrically opposed to each other.

Such divided communities, through their conflicting ways of acting and the messy situations they find themselves in are, according to Lonergan, 'headed for disaster.. For the messy situation is diagnosed differently by the divided community; action is ever more at cross-purposes; and the situation becomes still messier to provoke still sharper differences in diagnosis and policy, more radical criticism of one another's actions, and an ever deeper crisis in the situation.'[56]

---

[55] *Method* 356.
[56] Ibid. 358

Community is built on *co-operation* and co-operation is only possible when it is based on a common understanding as well as a common mode of operation. This inevitably calls for on-going change. If individual change is difficult, community change is even more so. Communal change takes time and raises complex issues. Examples of such difficulties are the conflicts that arise between individual freedom or personal fundamental option, and the group's fundamental option. For instance if an individual feels they have a right to act in a particular manner, and that right is clearly not perceived as part of the community's ethos or general way of acting, then this conflict, especially if on essential matters, must be resolved.

Co-operation is best achieved through *dialogue*. If a satisfactory answer is not achieved community may no longer exist. *Communication* is thus a key factor in both forming and holding communities together. Common understandings, judgements and decisions can only be brought about through communication that is on-going. The general tenor of what is actually communicated in communities is of vital importance. For instance is the currency of the community's verbal and non-verbal communication concerned largely with grievances? Or is the heart of what circulates between members as well as the community's relationships with those outside the community centred on goodness and kindness to all?

All change should in some way lead to greater *openness*: being open to new experiences/ new data; new understandings - those that are fuller and more penetrating; new judgements based on broader and more accurate perspectives; and new decisions that eliminate foolish opposition. Such changes, as Lonergan reminds us, call for change in the way people feel, think and act.

Fundamental to community is the notion of *authenticity*.[57] This calls for authenticity on three levels - the authenticity of the individual, the authenticity of the community's present way of life and the authenticity of the community's tradition. The struggle at all times is the combating of inauthenticity. The courageous seek remedies, the less courageous tend sadly to settle for leaving things as they are. The former are the representatives of progress and their method

---

[57] Authentic means what is true, Inauthentic means what is not true.

is that of self-sacrificing love which alone has the power of undoing decline in the community. Lonergan stresses that we only attain authenticity by fidelity to the fourfold operations of experiencing, understanding, judging and deciding.

Scripture and Community

The *Hebrew-Christian tradition* is based on community being a fundamental reality. God chose Abraham and his descendants, in other words a people, rather than a collection of individuals. To this people He revealed himself: 'I Am who I Am' (Ex 3:14). He also promised that he would be intimately with his people.

Jesus took this teaching further. He called disciples who as a group were to be his followers. They would continue his work of building the Kingdom as a group - the ecclesia or gathering. He promised to remain with his group of followers until the end of time. Just before his death he gave them the New Commandment. (see Jn 13:34, 15:12 and 17:21f). The oneness or bond that was to unite members of ths community with each other was to be based on the precept: 'love one another; just as I have loved you' (Jn 13:34). This form of love, was and is, the key sign of being a disciple of Jesus and a member of his community.

In the *early Church* we see the community dimension strongly in focus despite the inevitable differences that occurred.. 'These remained faithful to the teaching of the apostles, to the brotherhood, to the breaking of bread and to the prayers (Acts 2:42). 'The whole group of believers was united, heart and soul; no one claimed for his own use anything that he had, as everything they owned was held in common' (Acts 4:32). The Church today is the continuation of that group of early believers.

Paul speaks a great deal about community. Unfortunately we misunderstand in translation his meaning of the word 'you'. It is so easy to read his letters in the singular when often the original is clearly plural. In the main he largely refers to or addresses the community not isolated individuals.

The remainder of this reflection centres on the church community and that community's experience as understood and lived within the Roman Catholic tradition. This is not intended to be divisive but rather to foster an ecumenical spirit between the various Christian churches. The ecumenical way forward is through respect for each church community's traditions. The call to understand and be faithful to our tradition, while at the same time listening and learning from each other is more likely to happen when it is based on the understanding that what unites Christians is greater and more important than what divides. Differences also call for respect as often they are the source of enrichment through the diversity they add to the Christian church - the one family or gathering whose source and centre is Jesus.

Vatican II

Today communities, groups, organisations, businesses, strive to formulate mission statements. Such statements focus on the core purpose or meaning for which that grouping exists. Vatican II attempted something similar regarding the church before this became the popular practice it is today. While not offered in a crisp statement, essentially the Council Documents concerned with church tried to discern what church means in today's modern world.

Two of Vatican II's most important documents on the centrality of community in the Christian life are *The Dogmatic Constitution on the Church, and The Pastoral Constitution on the Church in the Modern World*.

The *Constitution on the Church* speaks of the church primarily as mystery since is it is 'a people made one with the unity of the Father, the Son, and the Holy Spirit'.[58] At the opening of chapter two, titled 'The People of God', there is the clear sentence 'It has pleased God, however, to make men holy and save them not merely as individuals without any mutual bonds, but by making them into a single people... Christ instituted this new covenant,... by calling together a people made up of Jew and Gentile, making them one, not according to the

---

[58] The Documents of Vatican II, ed. W. Abbott, (New York: Guild Press 1966). Dogmatic Constitution on the Church, *Lumen Gentium*, par. 4.

flesh but in the Spirit. This was to be the new People of God'.[59]

The *Constitution of the Church in the Modern World* is the only council document to have originated from a suggestion made from the floor of the council. In other words it sprang directly from the community of the Council Fathers. The thrust of the document is that the Church places herself at the service of the community of all men and women. Not only does the document say: 'our hearts embrace also those brothers and communities not yet living with us in full communion' but it includes its strong link with all humankind saying: 'this community realizes that it is truly and intimately linked with mankind and its history.... This Council can provide no more eloquent proof of its solidarity with the entire human family with which it is bound up, as well as its respect and love for that family than by engaging with it in conversation about these various problems.'[60]

This service of the church to the world is best carried out when the community dimension is manifest. 'What does the most to reveal God's presence, however, is the brotherly charity of the faithful who are united in spirit as they work together for the faith of the gospel and who prove themselves a sign of unity'.[61] Jesus stated that the purpose of his mission was 'to gather together in unity the scattered children of God' (Jn 11:52), in other words everyone. And he promised 'where two or three meet in my name, I shall be there with them' (Mt 18:20).

The Church Community: Pilgrim Church, Church of Sinners

This section views the church under two aspects of her life which seem particularly relevant today. These are that the church is built on the notion that we are a community of pilgrims and also that the church is a community of sinners - those who sin gravely and others whose sins are less grave.

---

[59] Ibid. par 9.
[60] The Documents of Vatican 11. Pastoral Constitution on the Church in the Modern World, *Gaudium et Spes*, par. 1 and 3.
[61] *Lumen Gentium* par. 21.

The Church is a Community of Pilgrims

Essential to being a pilgrim is to keep moving and not settle down for lengthy periods. Pilgrimage becomes easier when we travel light, namely when we avoid exterior and interior clutter. This is done by constantly letting go of what is not necessary for the journey.

The church is always on the move in the process of becoming more truly church in each period of history. This inevitably requires change. Newman's famous saying 'To live is to change, to become perfect is to have changed often,'[62] is a statement that applies to communities as well as to individuals. The church is the presence of Christ in this world. As culture changes so too must church in order that Christ's presence is visible within the new culture.

The church will not and may not change in essentials if she is to remain true to the gospel. However many aspects of the church's life do require changing if it's fundamental meanings are to appear relevant. The church is always in need of renewal as it adjusts it's method of preaching and practice to the needs of modern society. Making community relevant to the deep longings of the human heart for community is vitally important.

Vatican 11 says 'The Church, "like a pilgrim in a foreign land, presses forward amid the persecutions of the world and the consolations of God" announcing the cross and the death of the Lord until he comes. By the power of the risen Lord, she is given strength to overcome patiently and lovingly the afflictions and hardships which assail her from within and without, and to show forth in the world the mystery of the Lord in a faithful though shadowed way, until at the last it will be revealed in total splendor'.[63]

The Church is also a Community of Sinners

While in the Creed we say 'We believe in the holy Catholic church' we also know it is a sinful church. Admitting our sinfulness is precisely the way we come close to Jesus. He told us he

---

[62] J. Newman, *Apologia pro Vita Sua* (New York: Doubleday, 1956) 128. (Ist ed. 1864).
[63] *Lumen Gentium* par. 8.

came to save sinners...to seek the lost...to offer repentance... to eat with sinners...etc. The continuous succession of scandals among church members, including hierarchical church personnel, has existed in every age as historical fact. All members are human and therefore sinful.

But the church is more than a merely human organisation, a human community. She claims to be the place where the presence of Christ in his Spirit dwells in a special way. While this gives hope it does not eliminate our having to struggle with the unholy side of the church which we experience both in ourselves and in others.

The voice of people who are outraged by 'The Church' can indeed be painful both for those who have been sinned against and those who hear their voice. This outrage is understandable and legitimate, especially by those who have been personally hurt or even damaged, and that offense is made worse if the offender is an official church representative. Yet there is also need to balance in some way the strong feelings evoked, with the fact that the church is human and always will remain a church of sinners. So an attack on 'The Church' as a whole, or not allowing the sinner even in thought the possibility of ever repenting calls for some consideration. Part of people's outrage comes from their expectations and such expectations can vary in their degree of truth and realism. When we realize our own sinfulness, like the publican in the gospels, it becomes more difficult to throw stones.

The teachings of Jesus on this point are numerous, for example: 'the servants went out on the roads and collected together everyone they could find, bad and good alike; and the wedding hall was filled with guests' (Mt 22:10). Jesus seems to almost over-emphasises the point when he says 'Go to the open roads and the hedgegrows and force people to come in to make sure my house is full' (Lk 14:23).

A biblical scholar writes: 'Interpreters of the New Testament generally regard the parables, taken as a whole, as among the most assuredly authentic sayings of Jesus. The parables express what is most central and characteristic in the message and mission of Jesus... The Synoptic parables reflect the first-century Palestinian Jewish milieu'.[64] This same author points out that the parable of the weeds and wheat (Mt 13:24-30, 36-43) and the fishnet (Mt 13:47-5) show that the kernal of Jesus' message was 'the time for separation has not yet come; there is still the opportunity for repentance. Jesus teaches that he and his disciples must allow the good and the wicked to co-exist and leave to God the role of separating them at the time appointed by him alone. Jesus will not, in his ministry, anticipate the work of God'. The message is clear - the question of who is saved is in the Father's hands. Jesus' mission is crystal clear. He tells us he came precisely 'to seek out and save what was lost' (Lk 19:10). He also insinuates that full celebration is not possible until those who are dead have come to life, and those who are lost are found. (See Lk 15:32 also Lk 15:6).

Tradition is also clear that the church includes sinners although the church of the first centuries found it very difficult to accept this truth. Their idea, as it is today with some people, was that church members should be 'respectable' people. An example of this thinking was manifest recently when some people did not want a sex abuser to have a Christian burial. At the same time sensitivity to the struggles of victims of abuse, terrorism, or violence of any kind requires respect. There are people who have difficulty in even wanting to try and begin the journey of even partial forgiveness. Forgiveness is always difficult and the more personal the affront the more difficult it is to forgive. Ultimately forgiveness is a gift, a gift won for us in a special way through the power of Jesus' death and resurrection. All anyone can do is to dispose themselves to receive this gift even if there is a certain reluctance at this moment in time in their desire for it.

However, while sinners are validly members of the church their membership may not be personally fruitful. The outward signs of an individual's belonging to church may no longer be a source of personal grace even though that person still belongs and may even practice their faith outwardly. The inner grace of belonging to church in its fullest sense is the actualizing in a conscious way the union of men and women with God and with each other.

---

[64] M. Boucher, *The Parables*, New Testament Message 7 (Dublin: Veritas Publications 1981) 53, 84-86.

Rahner speaks of sinners in the church and the sinful church. He points out it is an article of faith that sinners, grave sinners are members of the church; they are part of the Body of Christ.[65] This is not self-evident - to some it is incomprehensible - it calls for faith. This incomprehensibility can be partially due to a tendency to over idealise the church and say certainly there are sinners in the church, but this fact has nothing to do with the real church. But the church itself is sinful. The church is not an ideal - what ought-to-be, but is a concrete reality. While it is good to be committed to this ideal the church is composed of all the baptised with all their sinfulness. According to Rahner, if the church 'is something real, and if her members are sinners, and as sinners remain members, then she herself is sinful. Then the sins of her children are a blot and a blemish on the holy mystical Body of Christ itself. The Church is a sinful church: this is a truth of faith, not an elementary fact of experience and it is a shattering truth'.[66]

Inevitably therefore, some actions of the church are sinful. However, the church is 'more than' its members since the Holy Spirit is indissolubly present recreating continuously the holiness of the church. Always and for all time the grace of repentance is on offer to every individual. We can go further and say it is impossible for anyone to live outside the love and mercy of God's unconditional love.

What is our attitude to the only church that exists; a church troubled by narrowness and scandals: the holy church of sinners? It is difficult to see how fleeing from this all too human church is the way forward since the church is and will always remain a fundamental source of salvation. 'Whether we want to or not, we belong to her and have sinned in her'.[67] When we weep over the sins of the church and our own sins and stand humbly before God, then God's forgiveness and holiness will shine through.

The church, and we are the church, while always constantly in need of renewal, is par excellence a community of celebration. Jesus loved to celebrate - especially it seems with

---

[65] 'The Church of Sinners' in *Theological Investigations* Vol. 6 256.
[66] Ibid. 260.
[67] Ibid. 268.

sinners. A favoured expression of community in Jesus' own life was table fellowship. This fellowship was inclusive - there were no outcasts. Indeed sinners and those perceived by society as rejects were particularly welcome.

We live in the post resurrection era so essentially our belonging to church is an invitation to an experience of joy despite the difficulties. The option is for us to help create that spirit of joy. The alternative is to live in a spirit of blaming others which was not and is not Jesus' way. Forgiveness is the true hallmark of the Christian community. The demand is to extend this forgiveness to abusers, terrorists, and perpetrators of violence in its many forms. Christian churches also need to forgive each other for the hurts and affronts they have caused. Community forgiveness is never easy and like all forms of forgiveness it is usually a process that takes place over time. The most difficult form of forgiveness of all can be forgiveness of oneself.

The Resurrection meals on the Emmaus road, in the upper room and especially at the lakeside were moments of deep joy and reconciliation. Now filled by the Spirit the risen Jesus reaches out to those who personally denied and betrayed him. All is totally forgiven. This gift of forgiveness is the first gift Jesus gives to his church on Easter Sunday. (See Jn 20: 19-23). This gift of being able to forgive others, even those who have profoundly damaged us, is now extended to all who can receive it.

Reflection

Ponder on what community actually means in your life.

Do you tend to live an a la carte form of Christianity or do you try to live it's community dimension by taking responsibility for the life of the church?

Do you offer initiatives such as ideas, activities, constructive criticism, or do you simply blame what you find distasteful?

Death

Sculpture

Cliodna Cussen titles her sculpture: Tobar - The Well. Wells evoke the notion of depth, the unfathomable. Death is the great unfathomable in human existence and hence this particular piece can be linked with the mysteriousness of death - one's own death as well as the death of every person. The water in the sculpture is an apt symbol of baptism which for the Christian means 'when we were baptised in Christ Jesus we were baptised into his death...we went into the tomb with him and joined him in death' (Rm 6:3,4). The cross is a symbol of Jesus' death; it is also a symbol of suffering in general. The ball, a circular shape, has been commonly used as a symbol of eternity - the reality that lies at the other side of death.

This sculpture is unique in this collection. It was chosen specifically in memory of Marie Webb who died suddenly in her middle years. Contributions were given for this sculpture by many friends of this remarkable women; friends who wished to gratefully and lovingly recall Marie's loveableness and most of all her extraordinary ability to love.

The sculpture is deliberately placed in a quiet, secluded area of the garden thereby offering a special opportunity for contemplation and remembering. The Mystery of Life in some strange way includes the Mystery of Death. Death, while incomprehensible and absurd from many viewpoints is also, as we shall see, a wondrous completion to the personal lives we have lived within human history. The Apocalypse speaks of the 'well of life' as the inheritance that becomes ours as we pass through death: 'I will give water from the well of life, it is the rightful inheritance of the one who proves victorious' (Rev 21:5).

This reflection focuses on three issues - dying, death, and the death of the Christian who dies 'in Christ'.[68]

---

[68] All the quotations from Rahner in these sections are taken from the following articles in *Theological Investigations*: 'Christian Dying', in Vol 18; 'Ideas for a Theology of Death' in Vol 13; The Scandal of Death' in Vol 7; 'Theological considerations on the Moment of Death' in Vol 11; '"He Descended into Hell' in Vol 7.

Dying

Dying belongs to our historical existence as we live in this world. As such it is part of human experience and so can be related to other factors within human living. In a particular sense dying becomes the experience of dying because it is perceived in the light of the event we call death and the dawn of eternal life that that brings.

In a more general sense we can say the whole of human existence is orientated towards dying and death. Death is a key dimension of human existence and its reality comes more to the fore in human consciousness as we move into our older years. Rahner says: 'this 'being for death', 'co-determines everything in human life and imparts to the latter its uncertainty, its openness to mystery and its ultimate seriousness'.

Dying in an extended sense is an event that takes place throughout our lives with varying moments of intensity. For example every time we let go of something, especially something dear to us, be it a person, through death or some other form of parting such as separation or betrayal, an animal, a thing, an idea, and step forward into the future without these precious possessions, we experience 'little deaths'. According to M. Kearney these experiences are 'death rehearsals'. Each time we cross these types of thresholds we experience a stepping out into a certain unknown - an unknown which can be made more difficult when the 'other' is no longer there to accompany us. Michael writing personally says 'I myself am crossing thresholds in my own experience. I am prepared, however falteringly, to entrust myself to the wisdom of my own deep unknowing'.[69]

So within life we live with death and dying and this comes to us in varying ways. This on-coming nature of death is consciously or unconsciously present in many experiences:

For example we constantly know our own finiteness for example, in our intellectual and personal pursuits. There is always a sense of limitation that there is more than we can reach. We also sense at times our environment and general milieu as 'letting us down' in some way.

---

[69] M. Kearney, 'Spiritual Pain'. An article given out at his workshop on Death and Dying in 1995.

Consequently, as Rahner points out, disappointment is a prevailing part of human living and this he terms a form of 'dying inwardly'.

Suffering and failure arouses in us an awareness that everything is not what it ought to be and this experience heralds death in some way. The general perishable nature of much that exists can add to our sensing things ought to be other than what they are. While suffering and failure can be transformed by an acceptance that is genuinely worked through, 'heroic' coping can never be assured in life. Neither is such coping assured in facing our own death. The only way to prepare for death to is to live well. Epicurus, the ancient Greek philosopher says: 'What you have to do to die well is the same as what you have to do to live well'.

The 'infiltration of death' as Rahner puts it, is more immediately felt as a result of serious and particularly life-threatening illness. Sickness always effects our whole person and can lead to a sense of helplessness. Rahner elucidates this point:

'The impossibility of completely foreseeing and manipulating sickness; the helplessness into which it thrusts us; the special, remote relationship to society into which it forces us; the solitude and the curtailment of possibilities of communication; the weakening of capacity for active self-direction; the permanent uncertainty of any interpretation of its 'sense' and its causes within the total structure of human life; the burden it imposes on the people around the sick person; the withdrawal from an efficiency-orientated society; the sick person's experience of being useless to others; the impossibility of integrating sickness meaningfully into a plan of life, and may other peculiarities of sickness make it a herald of death.'[70]

Despite our unknowingness and our general state of fragility, and the fragility of the world we live in, we do have the choice in life to accept the little deaths as well as death itself or, alternatively, to protest against our ongoing dying moments and our own death. While death

---

[70] This passage needs to be balanced with a more positive attitude towards serious illness. See C. McCann, *Falling in Love with Life, An Understanding of Ageing* (Dublin: Eleona Press 1997) especially chapter 4, 'Living Positively with Disablements'. This author disagrees in particular with the statement about 'the impossibility of integrating sickness meaningfully into a plan of life'.

in its final sense is a familiar occurrence it is always at the same time something dark and mysterious since death is the great unknown for all of us.

In the first reflection we saw that questioning is one of the human person's most basic qualities. Death calls everything into question and this includes enduring the question of what the true nature of death really is. Rilke, the poet, in a different context talks of 'a question to be lived'. Death is *the* question to be lived since its inner nature will always remain a question for us.

From the above we can see that dying and death are not events that solely comes at the end of life. The varying choices we make regarding our little deaths as well as our general opting for or rejecting positive values, make up our fundamental option or stance we take towards life. Death itself, as will be seen later, is at its deepest level the 'definitive end of the history of freedom', or as Rahner puts it elsewhere 'With death comes the finality of man's basic option'. When dying is over and death has taken place the time of choice is over. Human freedom has now completed it's history.

Death

In some strange way our own personal history seeks its own consummation just as history per se is not intended to be prolonged indefinitely. It demands by its very nature a 'rounding off'. Death is precisely the event when our earthly life is 'rounded off'. The latter phrase is echoed in Shakespeare's line: 'our little life is rounded with a sleep'.

Why, when, how, what happens are the many questions that surround death. Certainly human death is something much more than a biological event. Today it is recognised that someone can be termed clinically dead while biologically alive, (in order, for instance, that organs be transplanted to save or enhance the lives of others.)

Just as human living raises issues and concerns that reach beyond our bodies so too does our dying and death. Essentially death is about human freedom and the incomprehensibility of

God. Indeed *death provides the ultimate statement about God's incomprehensibility* and this is why death is for us something as incomprehensible as God himself. 'The death of man consists in the immediate confrontation of man, together with the whole of his history as a free person now consummated and complete, with the absolute mystery, with God', says Rahner. He then adds these powerful words: 'the truth we are pointing to is always the fact that death brings man into the presence of God, God who does not permit the personal history of man as rounded off and completed to fall into nothingness'.

Part of the problem is that when we grapple with the death question and 'life after death' we have difficulty in letting go temporal and spatial concepts. Time and space are limiting factors and death in bringing an end to both releases us from these forms of limitation. Death is not therefore a 'place'; a place where there is, as some people insinuate, ever more of all the good things such as joy, peace, love etc. Nor does the question of 'forever' arise, in the sense that things go on and on. Rather death is the happening that brings about a state of completion and immediacy to God. We cannot comprehend this with our thoughts - only hope makes this reality a possibility for us.

An alive hope does not necessarily take away an individual's natural fear of death and dying. Such fear does not mean either that faith is necessarily lacking. Learning to manage this fear by our attempts to find personal meaning in death is important not only for oneself but for others and especially the young. E. Ericson, the psychoanalyst says: 'that only in a society in which the old do not fear death, will the young be able not to fear life. Put another way, it could be stated that only in a society in which the old find meaning in their lives, will the young have confidence in any meanings they may be offered'.

D e a t h   c l o s e s   t h e   h i s t o r y   o f   h u m a n   f r e e d o m
An understanding of human freedom lies at the core of our attempts to understand the mystery of death. Rahner points out that the 'after life' is 'the finality of this earthly life and its subject possessing it in freedom'. It is not a question of the soul 'going on' after the death of the body. The whole person is radically affected by death. Our earthly history is ended by

death and this results in our person existing in a state of permanency before God.

Animals are blind to their approaching death but we are aware of it. We can take nothing with us except the radical decision of our own heart that opts for, or rejects goodness. An individual's fundamental option over their more recent life rather than their choice at the moment of clinical death is likely to be a truer indicator of whether an individual's freedom terminates in choosing the good/ God, or whether their choice has been one of rejecting the good/God.

Death is essentially that act of freedom in which our whole life is gathered up in this final decision. It is that event which allows the deepest desire of human freedom to achieve its goal. Personal freedom is no longer necessary since freedom does not ultimately consist in a quest to achieve ever fresh changes of will. Rather it is something that is freely achieved once and for all. Human freedom is always precarious; *death*, on the other hand, *gives birth to what endures*.

Freedom, Rahner says 'is not the ability to do or to omit one thing or another' but rather is the person's basic condition which allows it 'dispose of itself for finality'. 'The fundamental nature of freedom is the opportunity of a "once and for all" disposal by the subject of itself, a definitive self-disposal.' The responsibility this places on our decisions is awesome.

If our freedom were infinite this would result in freedom becoming less significant since all decisions would have an irrelevancy about them since they could continuously be changed. Freedom is that unique gift given to humanity. It is exercised in the course of the ordinary routine of life and the choices it enables us to make renders possible the rich state of bliss in the 'after life'. Endless finite opportunities to exercise freedom can never compare with the final act of freedom in death where we surrender ourselves finally for or against God. *Freedom achieves its own fullness in death.* If that freedom is exercised for God then a state of permanent face to face encounter with God is the outcome. This fact must surely enhance the radical value we place on our freedom in this life.

We are aware that our freedom is finite since it is under our control. But we are also aware it is something we are given - given by the Transcendent Other/ God. Death is the moment of final self-determination as well as the moment when we dispose of this gift of freedom.

Ultimately death has the character of hiddeness and this brings with it the sense of powerlessness. This powerlessness includes our not knowing with certainty whether we have accepted death or not. Living with the hope that death involves the approach of God's incomprehensible mystery makes our acceptance more possible and also lessens the absurdity of death and the experience of it as something that ought not to be. The real punishment of sin and sin's relation to death is, according to Rahner, this hiddeness of death. The light of what is revealed in Jesus' own death lessens that hiddeness considerably to one who has faith.

Jesus' Death; Death as Dying with Jesus

The Death of Jesus

'Jesus gave a loud cry and breathed his last....He [Joseph] took Jesus down from the cross wrapped him in the shroud and laid him in a tomb'(Mk 15: 37,46).

The fact of Jesus' own death reveals, in the most concrete way possible, that he was truly man. Like all of us he entered fully into the mystery of death. 'He made death his own act in which he accepts the inconceivable which is beyond all human control' says Rahner.

Jesus showed clearly in the manner of his dying how even the most precious things in life can collapse into ruins as death approaches. His cry 'My God, why have you forsaken me?' (Mt 27:47) shows how even God seems to have disappeared as a reality within his experience. He appears to have died cruelly and unconsoled.

The mystery we profess in the creed *He descended into hell* is more precisely put as he descended into the realm of the dead. It is a statement which declares that Jesus truly did die.

Peter in his first sermon emphasises the fact that Jesus' death was a real death. Death and being in a state of death are not distinct realities but the two terms help to throw light on each other.

Life and death interpenetrate each other. As the experience of dying is not alien to us in the many 'little deaths' we experience during life, so too the experience of death itself is not entirely foreign. For instance: we sense at times a great distance between ourselves and things of this world; when we descend into the depths of ourselves and struggle, possibly with the meaning of life and experience the poverty of our being, we have a glimpse, a foretaste of death. Jesus in his 'state of being dead', which we celebrate on Holy Saturday, enables us to see further into the depths of Jesus descent into human existence. The interpenetration of life and death manifested in Jesus' descent into hell has a value in speaking to us when we are plunged into the deep, dark moments in our present existence.

All our feebleness and pain, the Holy Saturday moments in our lives, have been in some mysterious way consecrated and redeemed by Jesus' 'descent into hell'. He has descended into the bottomless pit of human existence's experience of betrayal, abandonment and utter aloneness and ultimately to the unfathomable reality of death itself. He endured the human experience of darkness in this life and the darkness of death for our sake and conquered. 'He who descended is he who also ascended far above all the heavens, that he might fill all things' (Eph 4:10).

Death as Dying with Jesus

Jesus' death redeemed death for all humankind. He took upon himself not only our sins but also our death and made it his own. All of humanity can now die this death. Those who believe in Jesus have the assurance this is so. For those who may not even know of Jesus but who remain faithful to the end and who do not curse death enter the death of Jesus. To accept one's death is in some mysterious way an entering into communion with him.

The deaths of both believers and unbelievers may be accompanied by anguish and incomprehensibility just like what Jesus' death was for him. The death of the Christian, despite doubts, can be endured and even positively embraced when sustained by hope. The manner of death is a given but a given that is affected by personal choice. The choice part that is ours is to be open to the possibilities that hope offers us despite the external and internal difficulties that may be present as we approach our own death or the deaths of others and especially those we love. Cardinal Bernadine made a choice: 'Some people regard death as an enemy. I choose to greet death as a friend'.

For mourners, as well as for ourselves when we reflect on our own death, there are the consoling words of Jesus to rely on. Before his own death he told his disciples: 'I am going to prepare a place for you, and after I have gone and prepared you a place I shall return to take you with me; so that where I am you may be too' (Jn 14:3). That place is prepared for everyone as a result of Jesus' death and resurrection. He assures us that he will return at the moment of our death 'to take you with me'. Jesus' healing of Peter's mother-in-law gives us a helpful and consoling image of Jesus, not only as he heals, but as he brings each one through the gateway of death: 'he took her by the hand and helped her up' (Mk 1:31). Most significantly of all Jesus tells us the place where he now is, the place to which he also brings us, is 'nearest to the Father's heart' (Jn 1:18).

R e f l e c t i o n

Take any part of the reflection that struck you and mull over it.

Reflect on some scriptural texts such as: Wis 3: 1-6,9, 4: 7-15, Is 25:6-9, Rm 6:3-9, 14:7-12, Jn 12:23-26; 14:1-6.

The Mystery Of Jesus

Sculpture

In this second work by Cliodna Cussen she speaks of the sculpture's drawing power towards its pierced centre. This 'being drawn' is a powerful symbol of the person of Jesus and his words 'When I am lifted up I will draw all men to myself' (Jn 12:32). This sculpture flows naturally from the previous one on death - not death perceived as end but as awaiting fruitfulness in resurrection. Jesus companions us on our journey through life but he also brings us through death to the fullness of eternal life.

This sculpture is seen as a symbol of Jesus and Jesus as viewed through three of the 'I am' statements which he pronounced about himself : 'I am the resurrection' (Jn 11:25), 'I am the way' (Jn 14:6), 'I am the light of the world' (Jn 9:5). Cliodna noted the spectacular change that occurred as the result of her chiselling. The moment she cracked open the stone's centre the whole work was illuminated by the light that shone through. It became utterly different since the brilliance of light transformed the stone from its core. She writes: 'The pierced shape and the change wrought by the light coming through means that the mass is completely altered'.

The actual material, granite stone, that is used in this symbol offers special significance. Jesus uses a psalm to refer to himself. 'It was the stone rejected by the builders that became the cornerstone' (Mt 21:42). Peter picks up this symbolism and says in poetic format 'He is the living stone, rejected by men but chosen by God and precious to him; set yourselves close to him' (1 Pt 2:4). Cliodna mentions the piercing of the stone. Jesus 'the stone rejected by the builders' was also pierced when dying on the cross. 'One of the soldiers pierced his side with a lance... to fulfill the words of scripture "'They will look on the one whom they have pierced'"' (Jn 19:35, Zac 12:10).

Introduction

Jesus, as Christians understand him, is the central figure of human history. The Christ event, as it is sometimes called, especially Jesus' death and even more his resurrection, fundamentally changed human existence and has done so for all time. Everything about human living and dying is now radically transformed.

Jesus is the mystery of mysteries, as D. Nicholl well says, and adds he is 'the man with whom humankind can never come to terms. For no matter how many times or in how many ways humankind may strive to capture Jesus, whether in words or painting or music of any other mode, he always escapes'. Nicholl then plays on and reverses Pilate's words and causes Jesus to say 'Behold man! Now you know what it takes to be a man'. He points out that we can only truly search for meaning when we allow everything in our lives 'to be measured by the mystery of this man Jesus'. [71]

What the personal experience of Christianity means in day-to-day living is different for each person. Christianity is fundamentally based on a relationship, a relationship with Jesus, and like all relationships each one is unique. What this relational experience can be, and is for many, is difficult to express in words. The following metaphor of rich red wine can help articulate when words alone fail us. The conscious presence of Jesus in our personal and community lives changes our living from something colourless like water, which is necessary for survival, to rich red wine which adds flavour, colour, and a sense of exuberance even intoxication to life. Wine drinkers say wine transforms a whole meal - it enhances the food, the conversation and facilitates a general sense of personal and community wellbeing. The presence of Jesus does something similar except his presence touches all aspects of our lives. The risen Jesus, just like the historical Jesus did to those who truly met him, adds sparkle and joy to human living. 'In his presence is fullness of joy' (Ps 16:11).

This reflection comes to the Mystery of who Jesus is through three of his 'I am' statements.

'I Am the Resurrection'

The Christian faith is founded on proclamation, the proclamation 'The Lord is risen' (Lk 24:33). Peter and the other witnesses of Jesus' resurrection proclaimed from the outset 'God

---

[71] *Testing of Hearts*, 223, 233.

raised him to life' (Acts 2:24) and that 'Jesus is Lord' (Rm 10:9).[72] Death has no longer the final say in human life; death is now the gateway to the fullness of life. The fact that Jesus is risen is the central truth for Christians and from it everything else flows. 'If Christ is not risen our faith is in vain', says Paul (1Cor 15:15). The church at the heart of her Eucharistic worship prays: 'He put an end to death and revealed the resurrection'.[73]

Transformation is a key word in attempting to understand resurrection. The paradox of the resurrection is that in one sense it left the world the same and yet in another sense it changed everything radically. The resurrection appearances show that it was the same Jesus. Yet at the same time they reveal there was something very different about him. 'He is not as he was; but he is who he was'.[74]

Transformation took place not only in Jesus but also in the community of those who believed in his resurrection. The church was born through the power of Jesus' resurrection; a passover had occurred for both Jesus and his community. Following the resurrection many changes were manifested in the disciples. Most fundamental of all was their altered attitude to Jesus. This flowed from their new understanding of who he was - he was now their Lord: 'Lord Jesus'.

Other changes were visible. For instance contact with the risen Jesus opened their eyes and hearts in a new way. Their hearts burned by simply being in his presence even before they recognized him. Pentecost would bring this new light and warmth to even fuller brilliance. Their psychology changed; joy and peace became the predominant feelings. Their joy seems to have been intense when Jesus finally left them in his present form. His leaving in some way made him more intimately present; it was a presence of a totally different kind; it was a presence filled with life and light. A new form of prayer also came into existence - it was now prayer 'through Jesus Christ our Lord'.

It was from this shared experience that the new community of the church was born. The first

[72] See also 1 Cor 15:3-8).
[73] Second Eucharistic prayer.
[74] J. Wilkins, editorial 'The Easter People' in *The Tablet* 11/18 April 1998.

effect, perceived early that Easter morning, was faith. John said he 'saw and believed' (Jn 20:8). It was the fact of the resurrection that John believed in. From now on, as hinted in Jesus' encounter with Mary of Magdala, in a garden, we grasp Jesus 'in the embrace of faith'.[75] In some mysterious way, through the power of his risen state, 'Christ has taken us up into himself; our presence in him is an identification in the order of being'.[76] We now live 'in Christ' but this is a reality which manifests itself only to faith.

The post-resurrection appearances of Jesus were solely experienced by those who believed. The acceptance of the risen Jesus today also calls for faith. Even an exploration of this extraordinary resurrection event requires a disposition to believe. This disposition can be shown by an interest in what is proclaimed. As believers we have a responsibility to proclaim Jesus' resurrection, to 'go and tell' (Jn 20:17) the Good News that Jesus is alive. Christian faith compels us to utter its message. Paul found it impossible to keep the message to himself, he felt impelled to preach the gospel. (See Acts 26:9-23 and Gal. 1:11-16).

Proclaiming is an introducing or inviting of the other or others to meet, 'to see Jesus' (Jn 12:22). This is often best done in the form of dialogue between believer and non-believer, or 'shaky' believer. It calls for humility on the part of the proclaimer and the realization that the other person is also graced by God. The Asian bishops at their 1998 synod said there should be 'no arrogance in the proclamation of Jesus, who emptied himself'.[77]

To make the risen Jesus credible to the non-believer it is helpful to alert them to the human desire for fulfilment since this points to the possibility that some form of eternal existence, which is what resurrection is about, is not unreasonable.

The resurrected state no longer belongs to space and time and so even the notion and certainly the fact of resurrection lies outside human experience. Yet we can somehow imagine

---

[75] F.X. Durrwell, *The Resurrection* (London: Sheed and Ward 1960) 207. Durrwell is a French theologian and biblical scholar.
[76] Ibid 210.
[77] Report on Asian Synod in *The Tablet* 2 May 1998.

a definitive transformation of experience as we know it in this life to be a possibility. There is nothing humanly speaking that compels us to believe the testimony of those first disciples other than faith. Yet is venturing our whole existence on the idea that our personal life is directed towards God, has meaning, and is capable of being saved in this radical resurrection way of transformation, outlandish?

'I Am the Way'

My initial response to this sculpture was to see it as a symbol of a way, a way through to something further and deeper. Jesus' portrayal of himself as the way to the Father sprung to mind. In a sublime yet completely human manner Jesus is the way in that he shows us how to live life in our present existence. By the way Jesus lived his own life and through the teachings he gave us, he showed us the way to become fully human. That way is aptly summed up in Bonhoeffer's words: he was 'a man for others'. He is also the way through death giving us some inkling of our destiny.

This way of Jesus can be discovered by focusing on two central realities in his life - his passion for the coming of the 'Kingdom' and his central teaching: the Beatitudes.

The Kingdom

The Kingdom, whether in the phraseology of Kingdom of God or Kingdom of heaven is used over a hundred times in the gospels. Jesus' central vision lay around this notion of kingdom. For him kingdom is about making the world a better place; making people more fully human. Many of the parables, much of his teaching, and some of the miracles were linked with this kingdom theme.

Jesus clearly disassociated himself from the prevailing understanding of kingdom. His idea of kingdom was radically different from the political and kingly model of his time. The values of his kingdom are inclusiveness, equality, justice, love. These values are lived out through correct relationships, where dignity and mutuality are uppermost, and by a proper use of power. This demanded a radically different way of life to what was common in his own time. Today the kingdom also calls for radical changes in the way we live our lives.

Power, from the kingdom perspective, is non-dominative. Kingdom power is the power of love as opposed to the love of power and such power is essentially used to empower others as opposed to disempowering them. An obvious example in Jesus' life was his denouncing of oppression in all its forms. Violating people's rights and crushing people psychologically are clearly an abuse of power as is destruction of the earth's natural resources.

We all have some power. For instance we influence others for good or ill by our presence as well as by our words and maybe also by our position or our knowledge. Parents, for example, have great power. The power we possess is morally neutral. It is how we use it that matters. The Kingdom's use of power is primarily exercised in a spirit of service and in a way that helps others. Gifts, talents, abilities, opportunities, are all sources of power. Hoarding these is an un-kingdom way of living. Our personal gifts are given not just for ourselves. Rather they are given to build other people up.

Enhancing our own and other people's lives is what building the kingdom is about. This is achieved by a radically new form of relatedness. No one is excluded from the kingdom. Everyone is welcome to belong and those who are outcasts for whatever reason be it sex, nationality, colour, ethnic origins, religion, status- economic/political/hierarchical, as well as those who feel themselves 'outsiders', again for a multiplicity of reasons, are specially invited 'to enter'. An example of such outsiders in present day society are travellers, refugees, Aids victims, sex abusers. The latter are outcasts even among prisoners.

'Entering the kingdom' is a phrase commonly used by Jesus. To enter Jesus' kingdom is to be committed to its values and passionately engaged in the processes that implement these values. This Reign of God is concerned with now and with here, namely with the world, the culture, and the varying situations in which we find ourselves living out our lives.

Right relationships within Jesus' kingdom are shown through their expressions of equality. All are

to have a fair share of the community, national, as well as the world's resources. These resources are not just material ones but include things like knowledge, expertise and spiritual riches. Those who enter the kingdom late in the day/ late in life are accorded equal respect with those who have been cradle members. Latecomers, as well as and particularly outcasts and sinners, it would seem from Jesus' teaching, will receive preferential treatment. Jesus puts it this way - they will be the first to enter the kingdom in its fulfilled state, namely the eternal kingdom.

The way we relate to the earth is also a kingdom value. Respect and care for all forms of life and care of the universe as a whole was very much to the fore in Jesus' teaching about the kingdom.

In summary: kingdom living calls for radical human living. This is achieved by daily working in our co-creator role of transforming all reality as we, and the whole of creation, move towards the twenty-first century and finally towards ultimate destiny - eternity.

The Beatitudes

The Beatitudes (see Mt 5:3-10) give us a brief biography of Jesus. They show us the principles he lived by. They give us insight into what made him 'tick'. They provide us with an accurate summary of the way he lived his life.

If we adopt the Beatitudes we will become like Jesus. To understand the inner life of Jesus requires losing ourselves in the Beatitudes. The knowledge this gives is an intimate knowledge since it now comes to us from within our own experience of living the beatitude way of life. Such experiential knowing allows us to enter the inner life of Jesus in a truly intimate way. Nicholl puts it this way 'there is only *one* way of coming to know Jesus, and that is to follow him'[78] and following him calls for a beatitude life-style.

Living the life of the beatitudes is the distinctive mark of being a Christian. They are more radical than the ten commandments which form the basic moral code of the Jewish faith. The Beatitudes demand more but they also give more and that more is bliss and bliss in this life.

[78] *Testing of Hearts* 245.

An alternative translation of the word 'blessed' which prefigures each of the beatitudes is 'O the bliss of those who are... poor in spirit, gentle, merciful, peacemakers...' Bliss captures the depth of the experience of those who truly live the beatitudes. Jesus knew this bliss in a profoundly experiential way. Indeed his prevailing mood was one of bliss which was the result of his attachment to his Father's will which became concrete for him in his beatitude life-style.

Whether the beatitudes are set out in order of importance we do not know. The first one does seem to be basic. This reflection focuses on the first three.

O the Bliss of Those Who are Poor in Spirit

Jesus loved life and lived it to the full every moment. He enjoyed people, he liked things and gave thanks for them all. But he did not cling to them. He was always ready to let go, to say goodbye, painful as that can be. All he clung to was his Father's will. 'He ate out of the Father's hand'.

He was totally non-possessive of people, things, even ideas. This non-possessiveness resulted in a great freedom of spirit since there was nothing that held his spirit from soaring. His non-possessiveness augmented his ability to share, to give things away. The depth of his giving was not only his giving his life for others but his giving what was most precious to him: his Father's love. His final prayer to his Father is 'that the love with which you loved me may be in them' (Jn 17:26). The most precious possession we have is the intimate love of the person we love most. Sharing this is surely the epitome of non-possessiveness.

O the bliss of those who are gentle

Jesus became aware, especially as his life unfolded, of the tremendous power available to him. He could have used that power for himself. That essentially is what the recorded temptations were about (see Mt 4:1-11). 'Be somebody, show yourself to the world, use the world's goods for your own comfort.' But Jesus never used this power to benefit himself, his family or the disciples. Neither does the risen Jesus use his power in the sense mentioned to benefit his followers today.

As part of his kingdom mission Jesus always used his power to enhance others. He never gave out to people or left them downhearted. The power that radiated from him touched people in a way that healed and changed them. Schillebeeck captures this quality in Jesus when he says 'In the presence of Jesus it is impossible to be sad'. Jesus also lived in a spirit of gratitude towards his Father, and when we live with gratitude sadness lessens or can even disappear. Jesus' own bliss was further enhanced by using his power to better other people's lives.

Today we are aware of many forms of power other than personal power, for example, political power, church power, economic power, professional power. Sadly all forms can be used abusively. Lord Acton's saying is pertinent:[79] 'All power corrupts, absolute power corrupts absolutely'. The challenge Jesus offers is that it does not have to be so. He shows us an alternative way of using power.

O   the   bliss   of   those   who   mourn

This beatitude is about the compassionate heart. Such a heart is able to feel their heart strings torn at someone else's distress. Jesus knew this world of the heart. 'He felt compassion' for the widow of Nain. At Lazarus death he cried. When he wept over the city he broke down with the weight of sadness for his people. Many other examples can be found in the gospels of Jesus' ability to feel with and for people. Jesus' truest, most intense passion was lived out in his compassion.

Normally only those who have had some experiential understanding of suffering can genuinely stay with and walk alongside those who suffer, just as only those who know joy can rejoice with others in their joy.[80] Jesus knew that suffering place through his experiences of rejection, betrayal, failure, disappointment, anger. But he also knew joy; his life was essentially an experience of bliss. It is out of this context of joy and suffering that we can begin to fathom the last beatitude which is concerned with the blissful experience that can be ours even in

---

[79] Lord Acton is an English historian
[80] For a fuller elaboration on the theme of compassion see Chapter 7 titled 'Compassion' in C. McCann, *Who Cares? A Guide for all Who Care for Others* (Dublin: Eleona Books 1995).

the midst of suffering.[81]

'I Am the Light of the World'

Jesus is the light of the world in many senses. The essential one is that he is the unique and universal saviour of the world since he is the fullness of God's self-revelation. In his person he reveals the inner life of God to us; 'he is the image of the unseen God' (Col 1:15). He is uniquely significant since he alone has the power to save us from our selfishness.

While the universality and utter uniqueness of this salvation is a core belief of Christians it is also true to say that there are other authentic ways in practice that lead believers of other faiths as well as those who profess none to this salvation. God's grace is available to all.

Since Vatican II there is a shift in our understanding of other religions. This is also a keener awareness that Jesus is truly 'the saviour of the whole human race' (1 Tim 4:10). Both these factors have helped to strengthen the belief that Jesus is the light that offers salvation to everyone. This salvation comes in diverse ways and includes those who opt for goodness, love, wisdom as their basic way of life. Dupuis notes that every culture and every religion yields wisdom in ordinary everyday living and says 'where there is Wisdom there is Christ'.[82] This echoes a phrase from the liturgy: 'where there is love there is God'.[83]

While we know factually that other people, including those with their own saviour figures, can be saved without having any knowledge of Jesus, 'how' this comes about we are less sure. Jesus is essential for salvation as Christians understand salvation. But we learn from inter-faith dialogue that salvation can be understood differently within different religions. There are no certain answers about how salvation comes to non-Christians. An answer we can live with is that the adherants of other religions, and those who profess none are saved in a way only

---

[81] The section on the Beatitudes has leaned heavily on C. O'Connor's teaching on the Mount of Beatitudes given over a number of pilgrimages to the Holy Land. Charlie O'Connor is an Irish spiritual director and retreat- giver.

[82] G. O'Collins review of J. Dupuis *Towards a Christian Theology of Religious Pluralism* in *The Tablet* 24 January 1998.

[83] Holy Thursday Liturgy antiphon.

known to God.[84] Possibly 'the experience of a silence surrounding the nature of God may be the starting point' for our understanding of this question.[85]

The 1998 Asian Synod of Bishops discussed the issue of the uniqueness of Jesus' saving mission.[86] They agreed Jesus is the only saviour but urge a gradual unfolding of that message. Jesus should, they suggested, be presented first as a perfect human being. Only later should the universal and unique nature of Jesus's salvation be introduced and this needs to be done in a non-arrogant, non-insulting way. They point out that while Jesus is the unique mediator of salvation, that 'does not mean that there are no other mediators' although 'in a participative sense only'. They note that this message of salvation can only be effectively proclaimed by someone who has had 'the God experience' just as Jesus did not start his proclaiming until after his baptism - a profound God-experience moment in his own life.

'I am the light of the world; anyone who follows me...' who follows my way of poverty of spirit, compassion, gentleness, mercy, peace and justice; who enters the kingdom by embracing its values; and who receives the offer of salvation by acknowledging that one cannot achieve it by one's own power, 'will have the light of life' (Jn 8:12; the light of life that finds final fulfillment in eternity.

Reflection

Ponder and attempt to answer for yourself Jesus' question: 'Who do you say that I am?' (Mt 16:16).

What actual difference does Jesus make in your day to day living?

'O the bliss of those who are poor in Spirit'. What changes in your life do you need to make to implement this beatitude more fully?

---

[84] Ultimately, by the grace of Christ. See *Lumen Gentium* par. 16 and *Gaudium* et Spes par. 22.
[85] This section on Jesus the Light of the World is indebted to J. Corkery's article, 'One Christ, Many Religions: Speaking of Christ in the Context of a Plurality of Religions' in *Milltown Studies* 40 (1997). In this article he makes this quotation from V. Brady (an English theologian). Jim Corkery is an Irish theologian.
[86] See Asian Bishop's Synod report in *The Table* 2 May 1998.

Eternal Life

Sculpture

This is the only sculpture in the garden by a deceased artist, Alexandra Wejchert. This link with the eternal surely adds to the symbol itself.

The symbol of a flame was chosen as apt to evoke some of the notions that we link with eternity. A flame such as is seen in Yad Vasham[87] and other public places have similarly chosen a flame as a symbol of eternity. This particular flame, due to the lightsomeness in its colour and weight, coupled with the amazing strength and resilience of the material which when sculpted into its present form evokes openness, upward movement and a sense of aliveness and radiance, make it a powerful symbol of eternity. Even the slightest breath of wind causes the flame to move giving that sense of aliveness while the silver colour combined with the metallic material shimmering in the sunlight produces a radiant effect.

Introduction

When we think about eternity we are thinking about our destiny as human persons. That destiny, especially as a Christian understands it, is an eternal destiny. Grasping what this could mean is difficult. Reflection on the mystery of God and the mystery of the human person aided by revelation and the use of imagery gives us some inkling of what eternity might be. At the same time there is need to balance such understanding with Paul's words, 'no eye has not seen, no ear has heard...all that God has prepared for those who love him' (1 Cor 2:9).

This reflection examines eternity under four headings: Old Testament development of an after-life, the image of flame, eternal life, and the resurrection of the body.

Old Testament Development of Life after Death

No really clear formulation of life after death is found until the Book of Wisdom appeared in the first century B.C. The Books of Maccabees and the Book of Daniel, written close to this

---

[87] The Memorial to the Holocaust in Jerusalem.

time, give intimations of life after death. Previous to that, while the Israelites did not deny an after life, they do not seem to have seriously considered it. After death people simply went to the abyss, the pit, or Shoel. People like the Canaanites and the Egyptians, cultures who influenced the Israelite people in their early history, were polytheists. They had a God of the dead who in some way brought people to the 'other side'.

As the Greek influence became prevelent from the 3rd century B.C. onwards their concept of body and soul and the notion of immortality forced the Jewish people to reinterpret their tradition in the light of this new insight. The Jewish faith was always aware that a quality of Yahweh was to be everlasting and their word for that, 'olam', was in their vocabulary from early on. In this first century period they were forced to reexamine their doctrine that the good were rewarded, in this life, or by extension through their descendents. How could this apply to the righteous person who died untimely or to those with no children? The author of Wisdom broke new ground in the following passage and includes the word 'immortality' which is its first use in the bible. 'The souls of the virtuous are in the hands of God... In the eyes of the unwise, they did appear to die, their going looked like a disaster, their leaving us, like annihilation: but they are in peace... Their hope was rich with immortality' (3:1-4). This hope was based on the idea that if God is righteous he would be no longer so if the righteous were not rewarded. Reward has now become the hope of eternal union with God. This new expression of hope applied to all virtuous people even the childless. It brought a major evolvement in Jewish thought. Their hope now is 'that great will their blessings be' (Wis 3:5) and such blessings reach to life after death.

Flame Imagery

Flame is a rich and complex symbol. For instance fire/flame is a symbol of the divine. Fire is also a symbol of love. These two symbols are brought together in the Song of Songs: 'For love is strong as death. The flash of it is a flash of fire, a flame of Yahweh himself. Love no flood can quench no torrents drown' (S of S 8:6,7). This passage uses the flame image to speak of both passion and permanency. The passage overall, while speaking about human love, hints at the the human-divine relationship and the intensity of the eternal dimension of the love that

exists in this relationship. The fact that love continues after death is taken up by Paul: 'Nothing can come between us and the love of Christ... neither death nor life, no angel, no prince, nothing that exists, nothing still to come, not any power, or height or depth, nor any created thing, can ever come between us and the love of God made visible in Christ Jesus our Lord' (Rm 35,38-39).

The more primary and basic the symbol, the richer the symbolism it offers. Words are particularly feeble in trying to understand eternal life so unpacking certain symbols can be helpful. The image of fire suggest warmth. Such warmth can attract, have a welcoming effect. Examples could be the warmth of an individual's personality or the warmth of a hearth. Flashes of fire, sparks, evoke a sense of aliveness, unpredictability and sparkle. Fires too provide light - a warm, lively, enlivening light, at the heart of which lies a glow. Fire can be fascinating and ravishing as well as invasive in the sense of having the power to consume.

The Song of Songs text claims that the power of fire is stronger than water when it says that no amount of water can put out the fire of love. A love that is truly intimate and passionate is the most powerful source of energy available to man and woman. Everything in life as we know it comes to an end, fades away, even realities such as faith, hope and freedom. There is however one exception - love. 'Love does not come to an end' (1 Cor 13:4).

Eternal Life

The image of a flame has been used to understand love and the enduring aspect of love hints at the notion of love continuing beyond death. Can anything further be said about eternity?

We can attempt to describe eternity's qualities and this has been hinted at when the words passion and permanency were used. Another word to link with eternity is that of *bliss*. It is particularly apt since a fundamental truth is that God wills to be our bliss. It is not our love for God that is important but his love for us. Bliss is complete when this love comes to perfection in us, (see 1 Jn 4:12) and this is what eternity is all about. In this eternal state we can say definitively 'no one can snatch us from the Father's care' (Jn 10:27).

Beatific vision has been a traditional term used to describe eternal life. 'Beatific' is similar to 'bliss'. What does the term vision mean? Lonergan describes the beatific state as 'knowledge of God in his essence', meaning bliss comes from the illumination that knowledge gives. Lonergan not only writes about intellectual or rational knowing but he also refers to knowledge of the heart and quotes Pascal who says the heart has reasons which reason does not know.[88] Could it be that this heart or love form of knowing receives a new prominence, a new intensity in eternity? And could it be that it is through this loving knowledge that we come to know God in his essence?

The *Little Prince* illustrates this point when he speaks of the inner illumination that comes from heart knowing: 'What is essential is invisible to the eye. It is only with the heart that one sees rightly.'[89]

The Eternal Dimension within Human Experience

Paul Tillich[90] offers some rich thinking on the eternal dimension present in human existence. He considers the notion 'becoming' that is present in us. This becoming must be towards something, have a *telos* or end. He says 'Everything temporal has a 'teleological' relation to the eternal, but man alone is aware of it; and this awareness gives him the freedom to turn against it.' All of creation has its telos and will in some way be part of eternal existence, as stated by Paul. 'From the beginning till now the entire creation, as we know, has been groaning in one great act of giving birth; and not only creation, but all of us who possess the first-fruits of the Spirit, we too groan inwardly as we wait for our bodies to be set free' (Rm 8:22-23). The Spirit's role in bringing us to our final destiny is paramount and hence the flame symbol can be used for both the Spirit who is Love and Eternal Life where love comes to completion in us.

---

[88] Blaise Pascal is a French philosopher and theologian as well as a mathematician and scientist. Another of his famous statements 'Take comfort, you would not be seeking me if you had not already found me' *Pensees* v.11, 553. is apt for this book in general.

[89] A. de Saint-Exupery, *The Little Prince* (London: Piccolo Books 1945) 70. Antoine de Saint-Exupery was an air pilot.

[90] Most the of the quotations in this section are taken from P. Tillich. The italics are those of this author. P. Tillich 'The individual Person and His Eternal Destiny' in *Systematic Theology* (London: SCM Press 1963) Vol 3. Paul Tillich is a German theologian.

Human life contains within it the experience of temporality and in some sense the experience of immortality. 'We are aware of the lasting and passing of things that exist... we attune ourselves to what is lasting of which we are a part' says N. O'Carroll.[91] She then turns to Voegelin who 'suggests we learn the difference between 'existing' and 'being': 'In existing, we experience mortality; in being we experience what can be symbolised by the negative metaphor of immortality''. Put differently we can say we are aware that creation and consummation are facts within temporal existence.

A person's final end is determined by the decisions he makes about that end. These decision are based, according to Tillich, on 'the potentialities given to him by destiny. He can waste his potentialities, though not completely, and he can fulfil them, though not totally.' We have the choice to reduce ourselves to smallness or poverty or to elevate ourselves to greatness or richness. The terms rich and poor, small and great are relative ones.

Religious symbols give a very definite either/or terminology such as 'being lost or being saved', 'hell or heaven'. These revelatory terms express absolute judgements which Tillich suggests are impossible if taken literally 'because they make the finite infinite.' He continues, 'a solution of this conflict must combine the absolute seriousness of the threat to "lose one's life" with the relativity of finite existence.' If God created all beings as something 'very good' nothing can become completely evil. While acknowledging the condemning side in the final judgement, Tillich speaks of the 'absurdities of a literal understanding of hell and heaven'. He also 'refuses to permit the confusion of eternal destiny with an everlasting state of pain or pleasure.' As human persons we live with ambiguity. For instance saints remains sinners and need forgiveness and sinners are saints in the sense that divine forgiveness is always there for them.

The unity of the human person is vital to understanding eternal destiny. For example the conscious and unconscious sides of us are influenced by the 'given' situations of our lives. Our becoming grows out of our interdependence with the environment in which we live - be that

---

[91] N.O'Carroll, *Virginia's Questions, Why I am still a Catholic* (Dublin: Columba Press 1998) 110. Hereafter *Virginia's Questions*. Noreen O'Carroll is an Irish philosopher.

our individual biological make-up, the social conditions of family and peers with the moral climate that this provides.

'Distorted' forms of life, be they biological, psychological or sociological will always exist and such conditions make persons unable to reach fulfilment of their final telos. Examples would be the death of children born or unborn; physical or psychological disease; intellectual impairment; moral or spiritually destructive environments.

Tillich suggests that if we only view destiny in an individual way there is no answer to the distorted situation which we are all part of to a degree. He states that because we exist and existence is something good, plus the fact that we universally participate in existence, then the least actualized existences, for example, babies who die and intellectually disabled persons, are in some way caught up with those who are more fully actualized. It is a common experience that we know ourselves to be a part of a greater reality. He says: 'he who is estranged from his own essential being and experiences the despair of total self-rejection must be told that his essence participates in the essences of all those who have reached a high degree of fulfilment and through this participation his being is eternally affirmed.'

Resurrection of the Body

'Resurrection' as opposed to the Greek term 'immortality' is the core biblical symbol that expresses eternal life. Participation in eternity is not a natural quality of the human person, rather it is a creative act of God. 'Resurrection of the body' is an apt symbolic phrase to express this fact. This term negates the notion of a merely spiritual existence after death. It also obliterates the body/soul dualism.

The resurrected body is described as a 'spiritual body' by Paul. According to Tillich a spiritual body 'is a body which expresses the spiritually transformed total personality of man'. In other words the whole of our personality participates in eternal life.

The resurrection of the body strongly affirms the eternal significance of our individual uniqueness. In this life our outward appearance is utterly unique as is our self-conscious self. The symbol of the resurrected body points to this unique form of existing being part and parcel of eternal existence. 'Eternal life is life and not undifferentiated identity'. Individualisation therefore does not disappear and neither does participation. In fact there can be no participation if there are no individuals to participate.

The self-conscious self is not what it is in this life since temporality is no more. In eternal life we become a new being, a new me; not another me, but a transformation of the old me. Resurrection is not the creation of another reality. Resurrection is essentially about transformation and this transformation arises out of the death of a person.

Destiny is a question for all of us whether we are religiously inclined or not. The uncertainty of our ultimate destiny remains for everyone. Attempts have been made to answer the inaccurate extremes of the threat of eternal annihilation and the security of returning to an eternal source from which we came. Other answers people have adopted are reincarnation or an intermediary state such as purgatory. These answers are unsatisfactory. For instance in reincarnation the individual appears to lose their identity, and the doctrine of purgatory, while an element of Catholic faith, poses some difficulty in its strong emphasis on transformation coming through suffering rather than grace. Purgatory is more understandable when it is seen as the human person's need to adjust to the initial pain of being in the presence of perfect love.

Tillich sees an answer emerging from reflecting on 'the relation of eternity and time or of transtemporal fulfilment in relation to temporal development. If transtemporal fulfilment has the quality of life, temporality is included in it' - but not as we know it. It is not a question of timelessness or endless time. The answer lies in Tillich's statement: 'time and change are present in the depth of Eternal Life, but they are contained within the eternal unity of the Divine Life'. For the one who possess eternal life, that 'eternal life is life in the eternal, life in God' Towards the end of his paper he says 'God, so to speak, drives toward the actualization and essentialization of everything that has being. For the eternal dimension of what happens in the universe is the Divine Life itself. It is the content of the divine blessedness'.

Looking at eternity from God's perspective we can sense God has a concern about his creation and particularly about the human person whom he has given the freedom in this life to reject or to accept their ultimate destiny. Creation is driven by God's love and finds its fulfilment when that love is responded to by each individual in a positive way. A creation which is only external to God and has no internal dimension within the Divine, would be a type of 'divine play' which would show that creation is of no essential concern to God. But the bible is at pains to show the opposite. God is infinitely concerned about his creation.

Finally we can say in an extended sense that eternal life exists in each now moment. Jesus states emphatically 'Everybody who believes has eternal life' (Jn 6.47). Eternal life in the teaching of Jesus is particularly linked with Eucharistic participation. 'Anyone who does eat my flesh and drink my blood has eternal life... Anyone who eats this bread will live forever' (Jn 6: 54,58).

These Time-Out reflections started with the Mystery of the Human Person but now ends with the Mystery of God and the intimate relationship between God and ourselves that is consummated in a state of eternal bliss. The extraordinary fact is that God's creation and especially his creation of woman and man and their achievement of final fulfillment is of immense significance not only to ourselves but also to the state of blessedness within God's own inner life. What greater destiny could there be than that?

Reflection

Reflect on I Cor 2:9. Jn 14:1-3.

Search for, or create a symbol that expresses for you
the Mystery of Yourself and the Mystery of God.

Link both mysteries together as you experience

them in your present life with the destiny that awaits you if you live in joyful hope of what is to come in eternal life. Draw, write, listen to music, dance, or find something that might express for you the wondrous mystery of eternal life.

Shekina Sculpture Garden

Sculpture

Shekina Sculpture Garden is situated in the beautiful Glenmalure Valley which lies at the centre of Co. Wicklow. It has taken seventeen years for this one acre garden to come to what it is now. The main features are: the stream which runs through the garden feeding on its way two ponds; a gazebo; an arbour and other seating areas to foster both prayer and conversation; the undulating lawns; the open views of Fananerin mountain and the lovely surrounding countryside. The most unique feature is it's collection of sculptures by modern Irish artists.

The garden is the context in which all the sculptural pieces are set. The designing of the outline, levels and colours of the shrub beds; the shaping of shrubs and trees; the creating of the two ponds; the diverting of the stream; the digging required to makes these happen; establishing the optimum settings for the sculptures and seating areas lead to the claim that the garden itself is a form of sculpture.

This reflection gives the biblical background to the meaning of gardens and the term Shekina.

GARDEN

In ancient Greek the same word is used for both *garden* and *paradise*. In the East a garden was and still is a place where there are trees, especially fruit trees. When water is also present it becomes an oasis spot. Gardens are thus seen as delight-filled, favoured places.

In the Old Testament gardens are a symbol of many things:

- *of divine blessings* which included God's intimate presence in his created world. 'God walked in the garden in the cool of the day' (Gn 3:8). The garden referred to is located in Eden. The site of this place is unknown. Possibly the writer deliberately used the word Eden which in Hebrew means 'pleasure'.
- *integrity and praise.* 'As a garden makes seeds spring up, so will the Lord Yahweh make both

integrity and praise spring up in the sight of the nations' (Is 61:12).

- *of restoration.* 'They will throng towards the good things of Israel..their soul will be like a watered garden, they will sorrow no more' (Jer 31:12).

- *of fruitfulness and protection.* Ezekiel gives a lovely description of a Cedar tree which manifests these qualities. (See Ez. 31).

- *of love.* The poetical/mystical sense of the Song of Songs expresses the language of lovers and the setting for the expressions of the couple's love is a garden:
Bridegroom: 'She is a garden enclosed, my sister, my promised bride'
Bride: 'Awake north wind, come, wind of the south. Breathe over my garden, to spread its sweet smell around. Let my beloved come into his garden, let him taste its rarest fruits'. (The garden is also in this book a symbol of Palestine).
Bride: 'My beloved went down to his garden to the beds of spices, to pasture his flock in the gardens and gather lilies. I am my beloved's and my beloved is mine' (S. of S. 4:12; 6:2).

- *A garden is a place of temptation/struggle.* Adam was tempted in the garden and succumbed. 'Full of wisdom, perfect in beauty; you were in Eden in the garden of God. Your behaviour was exemplary from the day of your creation until the day when evil was first found in you' (Ez 28:12-18). The couple are banished from this paradise, but in the last days God will transform our cosmos into a garden of Eden. 'Yahweh has pity on all her ruins; turns her desolation into the sound of music.' (See Ez 36:35 and Is 51:3).

In the New Testament, gardens are also places of significance:

- Jesus gave his intimate teachings to his disciples, possibly including the Our Father, on the Mount of Olives, a place of many trees, at a spot known in the early church as the Eleona cave.[92]

---

[92] The Eleona cave and the happenings connected with it are mentioned by Egeria in her diary. She was a nun who went on pilgrimage to the Holy Land in the fourth century.

- At Gethsemane the garden became for Jesus a place of struggle. As the new Adam he overcame the temptation and accepted the suffering that lay ahead. 'Jesus left with his disciples and crossed the Kedron valley. There was a garden there and he went into it with his disciples' (Jn 18:1).

- The events of Jesus' burial and resurrection took place in a garden. 'At the place where he had been crucified there was a garden, and in this garden a new tomb in which no one had yet been laid...they laid Jesus there' (Jn 19:41).

- A description of Jesus' first Resurrection appearance to Mary Magdalen says she mistook 'him to be the gardener' (Jn 20:15).

Reflection

What are gardens for, what are they for me?

- a place for exploration? for challenge? for prayer? for renewal? for withdrawing? for reaching out? for sharing more intimately with others? a place for rest, relaxation, togetherness, enjoyment, celebration, picnics?

- a place for struggling like Adam and Jesus? Work in a garden is a struggle, a struggle that is always on-going just as our personal work of growing in love is also on-going. A garden needs continuous taming just as we do.

- Stroll around this garden or your own garden, or ponder a plant in your house and open your senses to what catches/lures your attention. Ponder what this experience evokes in yourself.

SHEKINA

The term embraces a rich Old Testament concept which brings together two realities - God's glory and God's presence. The symbols of this glory and presence were the *cloud* and the *pillar of fire*. The people of God knew God was with them wherever they were, either journeying or in specific places, through both of these symbols.

Shekina is an umbrella term that is used to describe both God's glory and presence as well as the symbols used to portray these realities. The word-symbol Shekina manifests God as not only the Most High, the Transcendent One, the Beyond, but also a God who is intimately close to us.

God's presence

We read in the book of Exodus 'Yahweh went before them, by day in the form of a pillar of cloud to show them the way, and by night in the form of a pillar of fire to give them light... the pillar of cloud never failed to go before the people' (13:21). Fire and cloud were two key signs of God's presence. Both signs were manifest from the commencement of their journey from Egypt and during their sojourn in the desert.

God's Glory

God's glory is a phrase which refers to the God-self. The glory of God is an epiphany, a manifestation of who God is. The term reveals in a special way certain qualities of God like majesty, power, the glow of God's holiness and the dynamism of his being. This glory was especially shown by God's interventions in history such as the miracles of the Exodus, as well as in the various 'apparitions' where the radiance of God becomes apparent in some way. For example Moses' contact with God was so close that the skin of his face was radiant. (See Ex 34:29).

The greatest revelation of God's glory was the brightness that shone on the *face of Christ*. (See 2 Cor 4:6). This glory was manifest in a paradoxical manner and to an extraordinary degree in the passion. Here intense beauty is manifested in *disfigurement* (a form of 'dark

cloud' where God was? Ex 20:21). 'Without beauty, without majesty we say him, no looks to attract our eyes... a man to make people screen their faces' (Is 53:2). Jesus' glory is supremely revealed when he totally pours out his love for humankind by giving up his life in the horrific manner of crucifixion.

The close connection in Jesus of glory and suffering is hard to understand.[93] It's profoundity makes it difficult for us to comprehend. As the poet T.S. Eliot says 'nature cannot bear too much reality'. When reality is filled with a great intensity of joy or pain we cannot always 'take' it. At such times there can be a tendency to run away, pretend such emotion is not there, soften what it is saying to us, or put off facing it to some later date.

God's glory was particularly made known to the people in three core events in the Old Testament. In reflecting on these events it becomes clear that God's presence and God's glory are essentially the same thing.

1. The great manifestation of God at *Sinai* took place in 'a dense cloud' (Ex.19.16). *The Cloud* is *the* symbol linked with Shekina-type experiences. In the bible the cloud is a privileged symbol for signifying the mystery of the divine presence. It manifests God's presence while also veiling that presence. In the natural order clouds are also a sign of God's blessing since they bring rain.

'Moses approached the dark cloud where God was' (Ex 20:21). 'The cloud covered the mountain and the glory of Yahweh settled on the mountain of Sinai; for six days the cloud covered it and on the seventh day Yahweh called to Moses from inside the cloud' (Ex 24:16).

The cloud surrounds God's glory. This glory seemed like a devouring fire; and the cloud is wrapped around this fire. Both the cloud and fire symbolise powerfully that God is mysterious. These are core Old Testament images which attempt to capture something of that Mystery

---

[93] The supreme revelation of beauty as shown in Jesus' suffering is an important theme for H.U. von Balthasar, a Swiss theologian. See *The Glory of the Lord* Vol. 1.

2. God's glory is again manifested when it fills the *tabernacle* where the Ark is placed. 'The cloud covered the Tent of Meeting and the glory of Yahweh filled the tabernacle. Moses could not enter the Tent of Meeting because of the cloud that rested on it and because of the glory of Yahweh that filled the tabernacle' (Ex 40: 34,35). Just as the pillar of cloud was with the people in their earlier journeying from now on the cloud went with them rising from the tabernacle. If this cloud did not rise they did not move but waited until it did.

3. We hear again of the cloud in *Solomon's time* when he took the Ark from the citadel of David and placed it in his new temple in the *Holy of Holies*. 'Now when the priests came out of the sanctuary the cloud filled the Temple of the Lord, and because of the cloud the priests could no longer perform their duties: the glory of the Lord filled the Lord's Temple. Then Solomon said: The Lord has chosen to dwell in the thick cloud. Yes I have built you a dwelling place for you to live in for ever' (1 Kg 8: 10-13).

There are two significant moments of this experience mentioned in the New Testament:

1. At Jesus' *Birth* 'the glory of the Lord shone round them [the shepherds]' (Lk 2:10).

2. Jesus' *Transfiguration* was a special manifestation of God's glory in the person of Jesus. The account of this event, as presented in the gospels, resorts to the imagery of the cloud in order to highlight that this was a theophany moment.[94] 'He [Peter] was still speaking when suddenly a bright cloud covered them with shadow and from there came a voice which said, 'This is my Son the Beloved; he enjoys my favour. Listen to him' (Mt 17:5-6).

This unique incident in the gospels reveals the early church's groping to understand and express the divinity of Jesus.

---

[94] Theophanies are moments when God reveals himself in a specially intense way.

Reflection

Do you have Shekina experiences, namely, experiences of God's presence in your life?

Are you aware of God's presence, in modern history, in your own history, in moments of special intensity (high and low) as well as in the ordinary moments of your everyday?

Attempt to open yourself to the possibility of making your Time-Out experience a Shekina experience.

Conclusion

In the Song of Songs God issues an invitation. 'Come into my garden, eat, friends, and drink, drink deep, my dearest friends' (S. of S. 5:19). *Time-Out in Shekina* encourages you to do just that - to drink deeply; to drink from the well of your own deepest desires as you ponder these reflections.

Appendix 1. The Meaning of Symbols

The first part of this section examines how we come to know what is real, in other words what is true, and also how we discern what is of value. The second part centres specifically on the value of symbols and the role they play in our search for meaning.

How we come to know what is real in life

How do we come to know not what appears, not what is imagined, not what is thought, not what seems to be so, but what is so?

Lonergan analyses in four stages how we come to know truth/ reality and ultimately value.[95] Each stage is based on the four levels within human consciousness:

1. *The Experiential or Empirical level* on which we sense, imagine, feel.

2. *The Understanding level* which uses the data presented to it from the experiential level. Our mind works on, inquires further into, our sensings, imaginings, and/or feelings, by drawing on previous knowledge, memories, associations, connections, in order to discern what a particular experience is really saying. In other words we bring in previous understandings to *mediate meaning* as we attempt to understand this now issue.

3. *Judging level.* Having sifted through the relevant data of level one and then collected the wider areas of meaning through level two we are then able to make a judgement: this is so, this is not so, or this is probably so, or probably not so.

In other words we come to know what is real through a world mediated by meaning through the processes of understanding and judging. We cannot come to full knowledge by merely looking at something. For example if we attempt to decide whether this particular item of vegetation is a tree or a shrub we first experience it - we see its shape and other details, then

---

[95] *Method* See chapter one. NB p 9.

maybe smell it and touch it. Then we use our understanding about what makes for treeness or shrubness. In the light of this fuller understanding we can then make a judgement: this is a tree, this is probably a tree or this is not a tree.

At the judging level we arrive at truth. The real is now in our mind; it has now become our personal truth.

4. *Deciding level* We evaluate the truth discerned in level three and relate it to choice and behaviour. We are now able to make responsible decisions in the light of the truth we have arrived at. This truth points us towards opting for value in the choices we make concerning our attitudes and actions. The final step is translating these chosen values into behaviour.

In summary: We discern what is true and by so doing make it our personal truth. We then make that truth operative in our lives in the values we choose. These values manifest themselves in the beliefs we hold, in the attitudes we adopt , in the actions we perform. Having said that, there is need to be aware of the heresy of relativism which says there are no truths but only opinions. Those of us who are Christians, for example, hold as true the truth of revelation brought to us in the person of Jesus.[96] We also hold as true that tradition has handed on that revelation to us through his church and that the central truths of our faith are expressed in our creed.

But each person has to personally 'own' or accept that truth. Truth therefore is something we discover ourselves. Like goodness, truth is not something 'out there'. Truth becomes reality when it is accepted personally; or by a group of people at which point it becomes a shared truth. Other people tell us something is true but that knowledge of others has to be sifted personally, through the activities of experiencing, understanding and judging, to become our own truth. Most of our knowing, is mediated to us through the knowledge of other people, since it would be impossible and undesirable to have to 'invent the wheel' every time. But it

---

[96] Cardinal Hume speaks of the need for 'a rediscovery of revelation - the ultimate truth which is disclosed to us of our origin and ultimate destiny'. 'Our restless society: finding a cure' in *The Tablet* 13 June 1998.

is still necessary to process that received truth as personally true.

The following example attempts to make concrete the foregoing analysis. Adults sometimes expect young people to own statements as true for them, and to make meaningful decisions in the light of these truths, without realizing that this particular young person may not have suffiiciently been able at this point in time to go through the stages of experiencing, understanding and judging and ultimately deciding on a particular matter. For instance meaningful religious decisions may be impossible for an individual at a certain stage of their life. In general if younger people are encouraged in their search for truth then the acceptance of religious truth at a later stage becomes more likely. Truth, including religious truth, can never be imposed. It has to be personally discovered and personally accepted by each individual.

Often we have difficulty in judging due to our poverty of experiencing (awareness) and our lack of working through the understanding process.[97] Jesus' challenge, mentioned in all four gospels, also hints at an inadequate use of our minds in our search for what is true: 'Do you not yet understand? are your minds closed? are you still without perception?' (Mk 8:16)

The four levels or stages of consciousness described *form one dynamic action*. This process happens spontaneously and largely unconsciously. Life becomes rich when we can make this process more conscious. Maturity according to Lonergan is concerned with discovering in ourselves what it is to be aware, to be intelligent, to be reasonable, to be responsible, to be in love. In life, we are always going from the known to the unknown. Humanity's search for the 'more' of knowledge and love is insatiable. To stand still is to shrivel.

A huge quest in all of us is to make sense of ourselves and the world we live in. In other words we *search for meaning*. This search for meaning is forever on-going. New knowledge often requires that we modify or correct our older understandings. It is a humble process but

---

[97] A. de Mello in many of his books points out that a diminished awareness and understanding of what is real is a major problem. In particular he sees this form of poverty as hindering the process of change. Change is largely brought about by altering our perceptions which needs to be accompanied by 'the willingness to think the unfamiliar, to see something new'. *Wake up! Spirituality for Today*. A video by Tabor Publishing on a series of talks given by de Mello at the Center of Spiritual Exchange, USA. in 1987.

a 'must' since the human person cannot survive for long in a state of meaninglessness. We need to find meaning in our ordinary everyday lives, as well as face ultimate questions concerning our origins and destiny.

This requires that we move beyond the world of immediacy, the world of the child, the world of pure sense knowledge, to the *world mediated by meaning*, where insight, reflection and deliberation are brought to bear on our sensings, imaginings, feelings. Knowledge is never found 'out there'. Coming to know involves personal work, whether it be concerned with knowing myself, others, reality in general, or God.

The value of symbols in the process of coming to know what is real

We need to:
1. Understand what is meant by symbol and the power symbols have in opening us to truth, beauty, love, meaning, as well as their absolute necessity in putting us in touch with the Divine.
2. Decide to expose ourselves to them
3. Become creators of symbols ourselves.

The Difference Between Sign and Symbol

Often these words are used interchangeably.

Signs are arbitrary - they are chosen by convention because of a certain aptness. For example red is used in particular situations as a sign of danger and by extension a red light is chosen as a sign to stop. Road signs, signs on food, are arbitrarily chosen to act as indicators which point to something else. For example stars on certain foods indicate periods of freezing.

Symbols are closer to what is signified. *A symbol is something, by knowing which we know something else.* Symbols are realities which allow something 'other' to be there, to be made present. G. Daly[98] strongly rejects the expression 'it is only/merely a symbol' since a symbol is always more than it tangibly is and says.

If the presence of the reality symbolized in the symbol is not recognized the symbol becomes merely a sign. Alternatively symbols can be erected into absolutes. For instance, when a symbol is confused with what the symbol symbolizes, in other words when a symbol is seen as the full reality then the symbol becomes an idol. Examples of symbols that can be interpreted in too literal a sense are the term 'Angel of the Lord', a Marian vision, the Devil.

The Meaning of Symbols according to Rahner[99]

Rahner says understanding the concept behind the term 'symbol' is not easy. He divides symbols into primary and secondary symbols.

Primary Symbols

Primary symbols are those which allow a reality to be present to itself. They are the outer expression of what a particular being is - a tree, a human being, God. All being, namely everything that exists, is symbolic in the sense that it expresses itself in order to be. For example God expresses his Godness in the Trinity. Put differently we can say the Trinity expresses who God is.

If God expresses who God is through a Trinity of persons, the human person - made into God's likeness also expresses himself in a symbolic way. An essential part of our existing is that we express ourselves to ourselves as well as to others. We only come to know who we are through our own self expression. Our body, our thinking, our feelings, our actions, allow us to 'be there'. The philosopher Decartes says of human existence 'I think therefore I am'. We come to know ourselves through our bodies, plus all the other qualities that make up the 'me-ness of me'. This means that part of being human is we are creators of symbols since we

---

[98] Gabriel Daly is an Irish theologian.
[99] All K. Rahner quotes in this section are taken from 'The Theology of Symbol' in *Theological Investigations* Vol.4. (London: Darton, Longman and Todd 1971) Chapter 9. Hereafter *Theological Investigations*. Karl Rahner is a German theologian.

are always attempting to express ourselves, and must do so, in order to be. Our body language, the words we use, the feelings we express are all symbols which reveal who we are.

Ernst Cassirer, a twentieth century philosopher, felt that rationality is an inadequate term in which to comprehend the human person and instead defines the human person as a symbolic animal rather than a rational animal since we are conscious creators of the symbols that express ourselves. Eric Voegelin, an Austrian philosopher, sees our ability to express our inner life as the distinctive feature of what it is to be human.[100]

Rahner's definition of symbol: 'Symbolic reality is the self-realization of a being in the 'other', namely in its outward expression'.
An alternative definition: A symbol is an outward expression/appearance of the inner essence of a reality.

An example which illustrates both definitions is the following. We would not know this is a tree, a dog, a person except for its outward appearance of treeness, dogness or human personhood.

It is important to note that the reality that the symbol evokes is always more than the symbol itself. For instance an individual is always more than their body, their feelings, their thoughts.

Secondary symbols
Secondary symbols are those through which *another* attains knowledge of something *other than itself*. The most genuine secondary symbols are those that can best express the other; whose reality can render another reality to be present in some way. For example Jesus chose the symbol of food and drink, the nourishment that exists in bread and wine, to be the sacramental symbol of his continued nourishing presence with us.

---

[100] I am indebted to Noreen O'Carroll's references to both philosophers on this issue. See *Virginia's Questions*, Chapter 10.

Rahner says *all theology is a theology of symbols*. God expresses his inner life in what can be described as a descending or ascending order depending on which end one starts: the Sacraments <–> the Church <–> Jesus <–> the Word <–> Trinity <–> God. The sacraments are expressions of the church, the church manifests Jesus to us. The order ascends towards the Trinity which is the ultimate expression of who God is. Alternatively we can look at these various forms of expression with God - God expressing Godness in Trinity, Trinity in the Word etc.

Spiritual realities like goodness and truth can only be known by their outward expression. For instance the concept goodness means nothing unless I know what is meant by a good act. A good act is the outward expression of goodness. Such goodness flows from the good person. Yeats sums up the value of symbols well when he says: 'a symbol is indeed the only possible expression of some invisible essence'.

Thoughts of Lonergan in Relation to Symbols

Lonergan points out that meaning arrived at through exposure to symbol can be richer than pure rational thought since it is reached in a variety of ways. For instance he stresses the importance of feelings in the process of coming to know. He says 'feelings are the momentum and power within our conscious living and without them life would be paper thin'.[101] Feelings are valuable indicators which help us discover truths about ourselves as well as truth in general and as such they could be termed our emotional intelligence.

Symbols are powerful means that enable us to awaken our affective life and this in turn has the power to transform our vision and our values. Symbols evoke the use of the senses, the imagination, as well as feelings and when these elements are combined with understanding and judging they offer an important vehicle in our attempts to discover meaning.

In contrast logic's law is linear and proceeds on a single approach, namely the level of rational thinking only. 'The symbol has the power of recognizing and expressing what logical discourse

---

[101] *Method* 31

abhors: the existence of internal tensions, incompatibilities, conflicts, struggles, destructions'.[102]

It is through symbols that mind and body and heart communicate and it is through this internal communication that we can arrive at fuller meaning. This bringing together of our rational and emotional intelligence adds greater richness than if only one form of intelligence was relied on.

This internal communication is further coloured by our *personal context* of associated images, feelings, memories and tendencies. We are also influenced by the *context of the society* we live in, namely, the culture of our age and habitat.

The Meaning of Symbols according to Dulles [103]

Dulles says 'revelation is inevitably mediated through symbol... [a symbol] works mysteriously on human consciousness so as to suggest more than it can clearly describe or define... A symbol is a sign pregnant with a plenitude of meaning which is evoked rather than explicitly stated'. When faced with a symbol we are stimulated to search its meaning. In symbolic communication the clues draw attention to themselves. We attend to them and if we *surrender to their power* they carry us away, enabling us to integrate a wider range of impressions, memories, and affections. Signs do not have the power to help us integrate in this way.

In symbolic knowledge a deeper degree of indwelling is required. To enter the world of meaning opened up by the symbol we must give ourselves; we must not be detached observers but engaged participants in what the symbol offers.

Properties of symbols as described by Dulles

1. Symbols give participatory knowledge as opposed to speculative knowledge, namely

---

[102] Ibid. 66.
[103] All A. Dulles quotations in this section are taken from 'Symbolic Mediation' in *Models of Revelation* (Dublin: Gill and Macmillan 1982) Chapter 9. Avery Dulles is an American theologian.

knowledge of a self-involving type. 'Symbols lure us...They help us discover the possibilities that life offers...By inhabiting symbols people discover new horizons for life, new values, new motivation.'

2. When we become involved with symbols they can have a transforming effect. Jung says 'a symbol does something to us, it moves us, shifts our centre of awareness, changes our values...It arouses not only thought but delight, fear, awe, horror'. An example of how symbols can evoke horror is a visit to Yad Vasham, the memorial to the holocaust in Jerusalem. The place taken as a whole as well as individual sculptures and pictures, and in particular the Children's Memorial, give powerful symbolic expression of 'man's inhumanity to man'.

3. Symbolism has a powerful influence on commitments and behaviour. It stirs the imagination, releases hidden energies in the soul, gives strength and stability to the personality and arouses the will to committed action. For this reason important social happenings rely on symbols, such as rings in relationships. Nations as well as political movements also equip themselves with symbols, for example national flags, anthems, crests, uniforms, and in the northern Irish context, marches and drums. Religions too have their symbols and such symbols can be things or happenings. For example the memory of key events in Jewish history are celebrated in commemorative feast days and this has led to the Sabbath and Passover meals becoming central ritual symbols of Jewish faith. The cross is the great Christian symbol. This symbol also recalls an event - the climatic moment of human history where Jesus revealed the depth of self-sacrificing love by his death on a cross.

4. Symbols introduce us into realms of awareness not normally accessible to discursive thought since they elicit from the beholder or user of the symbol, not only the power of the mind but also feelings, the imagination and the senses. Symbolic language allows us to cram in more meaning than ordinary words offer. Such language implies, suggests, evokes what lies beyond the words themselves.

A Summary of the Core Characteristics and Key Effects of Symbols

Core Characteristics:

- A core characteristic is that *the gap between what is seen and unseen will always be present.* Symbols lead to something further, deeper, richer in meaning, beauty, truth etc. For example the Eucharist is symbol which allows us to meet Jesus and Jesus is the symbol that leads us to the Trinity.

- Symbols *summon us to seek their significance.* They evoke in us questions as to what a particular symbol, be it word, action, ritual, gesture, or object, is opening us to. An example of a ritual symbol for Irish people is the St. Patrick's Day parade which is held not only in Ireland but also in other countries.

- Symbols *confront us to make a decision about the reality they present to us.* The choice, our personal response to what they open for us, is ours. We are free to accept or refuse what they elicit in us.

Key Effects:

- they conceal while at the same time assist revelation
- they open up levels of reality which otherwise are closed to us
- they unlock dimensions of our soul and always involve an ingredient of mystery
- they disclose not by presenting their meaning for inspection but by drawing us into their own movement and by carrying us outside of ourselves.

Symbols as Carriers of Religious Meaning

Symbols are particularly significant as carriers of religious meaning since symbols interpret the unknown through analogy of the known. For example fire is used a lot in the Old Testament as a symbol of the divine. Jesus uses symbols like living water, bread, light, to reveal who he is. While we must use analogies when coming to know the divine, it is important to note that God is more unlike than like any symbol we use of God.

Religion is often presented in a purely intellectual manner. Indeed we have tended to understand, look for meaning, including religious meaning, in too conceptual, too heady a way. Attempting to fathom meaning of the rich complex reality of human life as well as divine life is greatly assisted by exposure to symbol. Why? *Symbols rely not only on the mind, but they draw on feelings, the imagination and the senses.* All these capacities together are important in coming to know religious truth, beauty, love.

The Bible and Symbolism

In the Old Testament, nature, stories, historical events, prophets' actions, use of numbers etc. are used in a symbolic way by sacred writers as a way of affirming God's living presence among his people.

At the same time these authors make clear God is very much 'other' than us. The incommunicability of his name is a clear symbol that God is uncreated and thus totally unlike everything else that is created.

The bible is totally non-pantheistic (unlike much in new age religions), while at the same time God is close to, intimately involved with us in all the happenings of our lives.

A distinctive mark of symbols is not an absence but a surplus of meaning. They give us a language with the power of suggestion. God, though beyond description or definition is real. Symbolic events, language, such as myths and allegories, help to mediate, albeit deficiently, something of God's reality.

In the New Testament symbols are also hugely important.
Jesus is the greatest and most unique of all symbols. In Jesus the symbol is seen in its most intense, most personal and most historic form. In Jesus symbolic form and symbolic reality are one for in him the symbol effects what is signifies. To see Jesus is to see the Father (see Jn 14:10). In Jesus the full power of the symbol is manifest - namely the power to evoke, to summon, to give meaning. Jesus is the unique symbol of the divine. The symbolic form he

chose was to be totally human, to be like us in all things except sin and therefore he experienced all that goes with being human, like vulnerability etc.

The revelation of God in Jesus takes the form of symbolic communication. His words and actions always suggest more than what is stated. His parables, the images he calls on, for example, 'I am the Good Shepherd', 'I am the Vinedresser' as well as phrases he uses such as 'the kingdom of God' are rich with symbolic meaning. His partaking in meals, his miracles, but above all his dying and rising, offer a powerful symbol of his love, power and fidelity.

Coming to understand Jesus through interpretation of the gospels, is therefore enormously enriched when we understand the rich meaning contained in all of the symbols.

Communal Dimension of Symbols

Symbols have a communal dimension when they are shared by a group. Symbols can also have a history which gives rise to a tradition. For example in the three monotheistic religions, tradition, until now, has the symbol of a paternal deity. Since religions stand within a social, cultural and historical context, the symbols through which humanity apprehends God can over time reveal inadequacies of expression which according to Lonergan need to be 'corrected by reinterpretation, by so modifying the symbol that undesired meanings are excluded and desired meanings elucidated'.[104] A loaf of bread, rather than a wafer is for instance a truer symbol of Jesus' Eucharistic presence; receiving the bread and not the wine is an incomplete symbolic ritual of Eucharist.

Another example is the symbol church. It means different things to different people. For some the word 'church' has become a symbol of the hierarchy or a building, Few see it as Vatican 2 does, namely that church is the term used to express the reality - the People of God. It also expresses the reality of Mystery - the mystery of Christ present with his people. 'I am with you always until the end of time' (Mt 28:20).

---

[104] Ibid.

Symbolism and the Sculptures in this Garden

Dulles says: 'The major biblical symbols are transmitted in the context of mutable secondary symbols, such as those employed in Christian art and liturgy. These secondary symbols, when they cease to make the intended impact, can be replaced by others, *freshly generated by the religious imagination under the impact of the central symbols of faith'*.

The collection of sculptures in this garden offers modern symbols that have the possibility to open people in a fresh way to the great mysteries concerning God and the Human Person.

Appendix 2. Solitude; Silence

It is recommended that Time-Out in Shekina takes place in an atmosphere of silence and solitude. The following reflections centre on these realities.

Dictionaries define both words in a negative manner. *Solitude* is perceived as an absence of people and silence as an absence of sound. Only in a spiritual context are the rich positive meanings of each term seen and experienced. *Solitude* tends to evoke the notion of space/place whereas *silence* evokes more an atmosphere, a state of being.

Stillness is defined more positively. Dictionaries use words like quiet and calm to describe its meaning.

Both Old and New Testament contain references to these concepts, for example:
- 'Be still and know that I am God' (Ps 46:10).
- 'It is good to wait in silence for Yahweh to save us' (Lam 3:25).
- 'Yahweh will always guide you, giving you relief in desert places. he will give strength to your bones and you shall be like a watered garden, like a spring of water whose waters never run dry' (Is 58:11).

- 'In the morning long before dawn, he got up and left the house, and went off to a lonely place and prayed there' (Mk 1:35).
- 'You must come away to some lonely place all by yourselves and rest for a while' (Mk 6:31).
- 'Jesus was silent' (Mt 26:63).

Solitude

As human beings we live in a certain tension. Part of the mystery of being human is that each of us is unique, namely, we are different to everyone else (finger prints and DNA reveal this). This fact can lead us in two directions. Firstly, to a harmful solitude where isolation, in the sense of being cut off from people, predominates and where self-pity can take hold, or, alternatively to a fruitful solitude which leads to an experience of fullness. Solitude can therefore be a sour or mellowing type of experience.

O'Donohue describes the plenitude dimension of solitude as follows: 'Solitude is one of the most precious things in the human spirit. It is different from loneliness. When you are lonely you become acutely conscious of your own separation. Solitude can be a homecoming to your own deepest belonging. One of the lovely things about us as individuals is the incommensurable in us. In each person there is a point of absolute non-connection with everything else and with everyone. This is fascinating and frightening. It means that we cannot continue to seek outside ourselves for the things we need from within. The blessings for which we hunger are not to be found in other places or people. These gifts can only be given to you by yourself'.[105]

This author also speaks of bringing courage to our solitude; to hear in it Jesus' much used words 'do not be afraid' and notes too that 'only in solitude can you discover a sense of your own beauty'.[106] He says too 'when you inhabit your solitude fully and experience its outer extremes of isolation and abandonment, you will find at its heart there is neither loneliness, nor emptiness but intimacy and shelter. In your solitude you are frequently nearer to the heart of belonging and kinship than you are in your social life or public world... Unless you find belonging in your solitude, your external longing remains needy and driven'.[107]

The sense of belonging to self, to others, and to the world is brought out starkly at the creation of the human person - 'it is not good for man to be alone' (Gn 2:18). The tension arises from the call to belong, while at the same time experiencing the call to live the radical solitude inherent in being my own unique self. True solitude eliminates this apparent contradiction. Uniqueness and belonging are the one reality in God's eyes. Positive solitude leads us to a belonging to God; an experience that opens us to being filled with Presence - Mystery - God, and this experience contains within it the whole of reality. Yet this experience can be a paradoxical one. For instance some of the mystics discovered that profound solitude led to an experience of absence, of nothingness.

---

[105] *Anam Cara* 130.
[106] Ibid. 135.
[107] Ibid. 136.

This positive form of solitude demands the practice of *stillness*. Here we find our deeper self and this leads to self-renewal. This in turn opens our hearts to others. Important forms of solitude are contemplation and also suffering, especially when both become sources of spiritual energy for oneself and others. Solitude in the form of isolation can be part of the pain of suffering since each one's pain is uniquely theirs. Yet it is also true that the solitude contained in suffering can, in some mysterious way if we allow it, be filled with Presence. Paul Claudel, the French writer, reminds us that Jesus did not come to explain suffering or to remove it from our lives, but rather to fill it with his presence. Personal suffering can also make possible a sense of solidarity with others who suffer.

Jesus discovered himself as Son of the Father when he went apart to pray. It was here also that he got energy to work for the Kingdom. But withdrawal on its own can become arid, an intolerable desert. It is only the meeting of our solitude with Plenitude, with the Divine Presence, that brings light, warmth, love, strength, joy and a sense of harmony and rightness about it.

S i l e n c e

Silence lies at the heart of solitude. It unveils solitude's riches.

It is difficult to reach inner silence. We need to create an inner atmosphere, moments when we remove ourselves from the noise around as, and more difficult from the noise within. There is for instance much emphasis today on stimulating children while little about helping them discover the silence within - a place where they can find strength and peace and learn to be comfortable with themselves. Night and solitude naturally evoke silence. For some both are frightening, for others they are peacefilled.

Coming to stillness within is about *listening* in depth to what lies deepest in us. When silence invades our being we find ourselves in a place from which we can best communicate. The truest form of silence is adoration - no words - being present before Mystery in this present now. A totally silent encounter is likely to provide the most adequate expression of our relationship with God. The same can be true of loving human relationships.

A. de Mello says: 'silence is not the absence of noise but the absence of the self''. He has written profoundly about the marvel of silence and titles the first chapter of his book *Sadhana*: 'The Riches of Silence'. The following quotations are taken from that first chapter:

'Revelation is found in Silence... To grasp the revelation that Silence offers, you must expose yourself to Silence. And this is not easy... Don't look for anything sensational in the revelation that silence brings - lights, insights. In fact, don't *look for* anything at all. Limit yourself to *observing* whatever comes to your awareness, no matter how trite and commonplace...

The content of your awareness is less important than its quality. As the quality improves, your silence will deepen. And as your silence deepens you will experience change. And you will discover, to your delight, that revelation is not knowledge. Revelation is power; a mysterious power that produces transformation'.[108]

Master Eckhart, the medieval German mystic, said there is nothing in the world that resembles God as much as silence. God normally reveals himself in silence. In fact silence is par excellence the sign that mediates God's presence to us.

Ignatius of Antioch, a second century church Father said: 'The Father uttered a word and it was his Son, and the Word speaks ever in eternal silence and in silence must the soul listen to it.' The book of Wisdom puts it this way: 'When peaceful silence lay over all, and night had run the half of her swift course, down from the heavens, leapt your all-powerful Word'. (Wis 18:14,15).

Silence is clearly a revelatory language and may even be its most powerful expression. The Mystery of Holy Saturday reveals the awesome silence of Jesus in death and the tomb.[109] This event in turn points to something very profound, namely the depth of his love in descending to the deepest, darkest, most unknown place. This 'place' of apparent emptiness and ultimate silence is transformed through the mystery of his Resurrection showing that even the most obscure types of silence can be pregnant with fullness.

[108] A. de Mello, *Sadhana, A Way to God*, (Anand: Anand Press 1985) 3-6.
[109] See especially H. Urs von Balthasar, *Mysterium Paschal, The Mystery of Easter* (Edinburgh: T & T. Clark). For Balthasar the kenosis of Jesus was 'a single movement which on Holy Saturday receives its supreme dramtic intensity'. 179.

Sources Consulted

The Mystery of the Human Person

R. Leakey, *The Origin of Humankind*, (London: Phoenix 1994).

B. Lonergan, *Method in Theology*, (Toronto: Toronto Press 1971).

V. Frankl, *Man's Search for Meaning*, (New York: Washington Square Press 1959).

Absolute Mystery - God

W. Kasper, *The God of Jesus Christ*, (London: SCM Press 1982).

K. Rahner, 'The Hiddenness of God' in *Theological Investigations* Vol 16.

The Holy Spirit

B. Lonergan, *Method in Theology*, (Toronto: University of Toronto Press 1971).

Creation of the Universe

The Jerusalem Bible, (London: Darton, Longman & Todd 1966).

L. Dufour, *Dictionary of Biblical Theology*, (London: Chapman 1970).

Creation of Man and Woman

F. Herder and J. Heagle, *Your Sexual Self*, (Indiana: Ave Maria Press 1992).

Mother and Child

J. Vanier, *Tears of Silence*, (New Jersey: Dimension Books 1970).

K. Rahner, ' A Theology of Childhood' in *Theological Investiagations* Vol 8.

Lovers

M. Buber, *I and Thou*, (Edinburgh: T & T Clark 1923).

M. Williams, *The Velveteen Rabbit*, (London: Mammoth 1922).

Community

Documents of the Vatican Council, (New York: Guild Press 1966).

K. Rahner, 'The Church of Sinners'. in *Theological Investigations* Vol 6.

B. Lonergan, *Method in Theology*.

Death

K. Rahner, 'Christian Dying', in Vol 18; 'Ideas for a Theology of Death' in Vol 13; The Scandal of Death' in Vol 7; 'Theological Considerations on the Moment of Death' in Vol 11; He Descended into Hell' in Vol 7. All volumes are in *Theological Investigations.*

M. Kearney *Mortally Wounded, Stories of Soul Pain, Death and Healing* (Dublin: Marino Books 1996)

The Mystery of Jesus

F.X Durrwell, *The Resurrection,* (London: sheed and Ward 1960).

D. O'Murchu, *Reclaiming Spirituality,* (Dublin: Gill & Macmillan 1997).

J. Corkery, 'One Christ, Many Religions: Speaking of Christ in the Context of a Plurality of Religions' in *Milltown Studies* 40 (1997) 5-30.

Eternal Life

P. Tillich, 'The Individual Person and His Eternal Destiny' in *Systematic Theology* Vol 3 (London: SCM Press 1963).

Appendix -

1. The Meaning of Symbols

K. Rahner, 'The Theology of Symbol' in *Theological Investigations* Vol 4, (London: Darton, Longman & Todd 1971).

A. Dulles, 'Symbolic Mediation' in *Models of Revelation*, (Dublin: Gill & Macmillan 1982)

2. Solitude, Silence

J. O'Donohue, *Anam Cara*, (London: Bantam Press 1997).

A. de Mello, *Sadhana, A Way to God*, (Anand: Anand Press 1985).

Notes